D0034136

NEXT LEVEL PARENTING

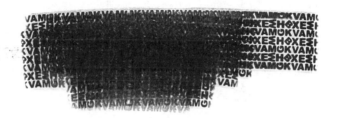

RICH ROGERS
"DR. RICH"

Christian
LIFE
A STRANG COMPANY

Most STRANG COMMUNICATIONS/CHARISMA HOUSE/CHRISTIAN LIFE/EXCEL BOOKS/FRONTLINE/REALMS/SILOAM products are available at special quantity discounts for bulk purchase for sales promotions, premiums, fund-raising, and educational needs. For details, write Strang Communications Book Group, 600 Rinehart Road, Lake Mary, Florida 32746, or telephone (407) 333-0600.

NEXT LEVEL PARENTING by Rich Rogers
Published by Christian Life
A Strang Company
600 Rinehart Road
Lake Mary, Florida 32746
www.strangdirect.com

This book or parts thereof may not be reproduced in any form, stored in a retrieval system, or transmitted in any form by any means—electronic, mechanical, photocopy, recording, or otherwise—without prior written permission of the publisher, except as provided by United States of America copyright law.

Unless otherwise noted, all Scripture quotations are from the Holy Bible, New International Version. Copyright © 1973, 1978, 1984, International Bible Society. Used by permission.

Scripture quotations marked AMP are from the Amplified Bible. Old Testament copyright © 1965, 1987 by the Zondervan Corporation. The Amplified New Testament copyright © 1954, 1958, 1987 by the Lockman Foundation. Used by permission.

Scripture quotations marked CEV are from the Contemporary English Version, copyright © 1995 by the American Bible Society. Used by permission.

Scripture quotations marked GNT are from the Good News Translation, second edition, copyright © 1992 by American Bible Society. Used by permission.

Scripture quotations marked KJV are from the King James Version of the Bible.

Scripture quotations marked THE MESSAGE are from The Message: The Bible in Contemporary English, copyright © 1993, 1994, 1995, 1996, 2000, 2001, 2002. Used by permission of NavPress Publishing Group.

Scripture quotations marked NAS are from the New American Standard Bible. Copyright © 1960, 1962, 1963, 1968, 1971, 1972, 1973, 1975, 1977 by the Lockman Foundation. Used by permission. (www.Lockman.org).

Scripture quotations marked NKJV are from the New King James Version of the Bible. Copyright © 1979, 1980, 1982 by Thomas Nelson, Inc., publishers. Used by permission.

Scripture quotations marked NLT are from the Holy Bible, New Living Translation, copyright © 1996. Used by permission of Tyndale House Publishers, Inc., Wheaton, IL 60189. All rights reserved.

Design Director: Bill Johnson
Cover design by Karen Grindley

Copyright © 2009 by Rich Rogers
All rights reserved

Library of Congress Cataloging-in-Publication Data:

Rogers, Rich.
  Next level parenting / Rich Rogers. -- 1st ed.
    p. cm.
  Includes bibliographical references.
  ISBN 978-1-59979-473-0
  1. ParentingxReligious aspects--Christianity. 2. Child rearing--Religious aspects-
-Christianity. I. Title.
  BV4529.R64 2009
  248.8'45--dc22

                              2008046825

First Edition

09 10 11 12 13 — 987654321
Printed in the United States of America

This book is dedicated to the four greatest professors of parent education I know...my four beautiful daughters, Lexi, Rachel, Mackenzie, and Skylar. Day by day, year after year, we live the miracle that is our family. I also extend my greatest appreciation and affection to my partner in the journey, my wife, Theresa. While we may not always get it right, we do always love, and through our commitment to the journey, we will see our children rise up and change the world—each in their own unique way. Jesus is our guide, and His Word our torch. Praise be to the God of the universe for His mercy, His grace, and second chances.

CONTENTS

SECTION IV PARENTING AT THE NEXT LEVEL

SECTION V DECLARE YOUR INTENTIONS

SECTION VI PEOPLE OF JOY WITH CHILDREN OF HOPE

FOREWORD

NEVER BEFORE IN the history of our nation has there been a greater need for the parents of America to wake up and acknowledge that there is a battle raging for the attention, affections, and very souls of our children. While there are many great books by great men and women of God about raising kids, few address the need for spiritual parenting the way this book does. And what I love the most is the way Dr. Rich breaks it down with practical strategies and a game plan that any parent can follow. Many parents have attended the Next Level Parenting seminars, and they are taking back their families by responding to the voice of the Holy Spirit calling them to a higher place to set themselves apart for a God-sized purpose that requires a God-sized commitment, resulting in a God-sized harvest. They have a dream, a promise, or a strong yearning to see their children worship and serve the living God as never before.

What Dr. Rich has done in *Next Level Parenting* is connect parents to a six-step pattern found throughout the Scriptures, and he walks each reader through the process God has used for centuries in the lives of those He has called to the divine purpose of parenting. Dr. Rich has taught this process to parents in our congregations with great results.

I have devoted many hours in my pulpit pleading and encouraging parents to fight for their family. *Next Level Parenting* takes that imperative and places the weapons squarely in your hands—chapter after chapter—giving you every tool you need to win the battle…for your child and mine.

—JENTEZEN FRANKLIN
SENIOR PASTOR, FREE CHAPEL
NEW YORK TIMES BEST-SELLING AUTHOR OF *FASTING*

INTRODUCTION

The dogmas of the quiet past are inadequate to the stormy
present.

The occasion is piled high with difficulty, and we must rise
to the occasion. As our case is new, so we must think and act
anew.[1]

—ABRAHAM LINCOLN

S OME TIME AGO, my wife and I visited a church in North Georgia
that would soon become our church home. As it turned out, our first
day at this church was the last day of a very special annual event.
Most of the members of this church had just spent the previous twenty-
one days fasting and praying, and as a result, they were believing God for
incredible things. As I watched and listened to the music and preaching
that morning, I could tell that this was no ordinary church. I could sense
God's presence and His moving in that congregation in a way that I had
not felt in recent memory. Later in the day, there was to be an evening
service where they would come together to pray for the sick and afflicted
and to lift up the many things that were weighing on the hearts of men and
women of God, expecting the Lord to move in miraculous ways.

Well, this was a bit beyond my normal Sunday experience, but I was
curious to see what God would do with more than one thousand people
who had fasted and prayed earnestly for twenty-one days straight. So that

night, my wife and I secured a babysitter and headed off into that cold, damp night to attend this service.

We arrived to find the place packed. More than fifteen hundred people in this little town in North Georgia had made the trek out to the edge of town to attend this service, and there was great expectation in the air. The service began with praise and worship, followed by an explanation of how the evening was going to proceed. Then they set up seventy chairs or so all around the stage and across the front of the auditorium while the leaders in the church all picked chairs and stood behind them, waiting to intercede for whoever might come seeking prayer.

The pastor first asked for those with physical ailments to come forward to be prayed over. There was a good smattering of people who went forward and were prayed for all over the stage and across the front. As people came forward and filled the chairs, the leaders simply asked what they needed prayer for, anointed their head with oil, and then prayed for each person individually. My wife and I watched, prayed, and sang along with the worship leaders as the worship service continued. There was nothing mystical or fanatical about the evening, just simple folks doing the best they could to follow Scripture and pray for those who had needs.

As this season of prayer came to an end, the pastor asked for those experiencing financial strife or difficulties to come forward, and many did. In fact, there were quite a few more asking for prayer in this area of their lives than there were asking for prayer for physical needs.

Then, about one hour into the evening, something extraordinary happened, and it became apparently clear why God had me there that cold, wintry night. The prayer time for those with financial needs was drawing to a close, and the pastor took the microphone and asked for those who were *in need of restoration or God's intervention in their families* to come forward. The response was overwhelming, as nearly the entire auditorium emptied into the aisles. I sat weeping as I witnessed firsthand the incredible need for God's movement, healing, and intervention in the families of America.

Three years prior to this Sunday evening service, God gave me the calling to write this book, *Next Level Parenting*, and since that time I had experienced numerous confirmations of that calling. But that night God gave me something else. That night God gave me *a greater sense of urgency*, while also allowing me to see inside the homes of people just like you and me, desperately in need of God's presence in their families.

I brought my first draft of this book to that service with the intention of lifting it up to God for Him to use any way He saw fit, and that is what I did. Right there in my seat, I dedicated this to Him and told Him I would go anywhere and do anything He asked me to do to sow His message and His plan for families in the minds and hearts of His people.

I believe with all my heart that the Lord has given me a message to give to Christian families and churches in America. It is not only a message of warning and instruction but also a message of hope and promise. The urgency is of utmost importance as Christian families all across this great country are flooding aisles of churches, seeking hope, restoration, and a plan for their families. God has all three covered and available to those who will stop, listen, and then parent at the next level.

What Is the Next Level?

As I described in my first book, *Next Level Living*, the next level in the physical realm is who we are when we are at our best. It is what is possible when we give ourselves completely to a cause. It is what we are capable of when we are trained, disciplined, and focused over an extended period of time.

In ministry, it is what is possible when people are fervently praying, leaders are going above and beyond the call of duty, and spiritual priorities have greater weight than personal privacy and leisure.

In regard to true Christian parenting, the next level involves placing as much focus and effort on addressing what is happening in the spirit realm as you do in the physical realm. In fact, more is needed. In my first book, I make a clear distinction between the physical world, which is what we can see, touch, feel, experience, and measure, and the spiritual world, which is not as easy to see, touch, feel, experience, and measure—unless you know what to look for. I cannot begin to convey to you the level of intensity that is being exerted in that realm by all of the forces of evil to wrestle your children away from you and to lead them down a path away from faith in Jesus Christ. If I could find the words to say this in even stronger terms, I would.

So, this is the common thread of living life at the next level—putting forth extraordinary effort over an extended period of time, which includes self-discipline, selflessness, being teachable, and the ability to see and live life and all its experiences through the eyes of Christ. These are the hallmarks of next-level achievements.

Parenting at the next level is not something that can be accomplished by an event, a trip, an afternoon, or even an incredible moment. But just as I said above, this can only happen as the result of extraordinary effort, self-discipline, and going above and beyond the call of duty *over an extended period of time*. Most parents can commit to the moments, the trips, and the events, but it's in the long haul that they are losing the battle. Yes, there is sacrifice. And, yes, it may demand a major overhaul of your priorities, but I believe with all my heart that the victory that lies at the finish line will be worth every moment spent and every sacrifice made.

My Commission

Scripture, in its final epitaph on the life of David, says this: "David had served God's purpose in his own generation" (Acts 13:36).

As I write this book, it is with this one goal in mind: *that I might serve God's purposes in my generation.* I believe with everything in me that the Lord has given me a message for the Christian parents of this nation and for the church that has been called to minister to these families for this generation. What follows in the pages ahead is the message God has given me to proclaim to this nation. Please read each chapter with a prayerful heart and an open mind, knowing that the Word of the Lord does not return void.

But as you read, please understand a timeless principle outlined in Luke that says, "From everyone who has been given much, much will be demanded; and from the one who has been entrusted with much, much more will be asked" (Luke 12:48).

Much has already been given to you in the form of God's precious gifts, your children. Whether you are a parent, grandparent, or a pastor of a church, this book is written as a message to you. It is part information, part rebuke, part warning, but mostly encouragement and instruction.

GENERATION NEXT

After years of research and studies of the impact of church and religious life on the life of young people, Christian researcher George Barna recently concluded the following:

> The moral foundations of children are typically solidified by the age of nine and life-long spiritual choices regarding one's faith and one's relationship with Jesus Christ are generally made before they reach age 13. Furthermore, a person's religious beliefs are usually worked out prior to becoming a teenager—and those beliefs rarely change to any meaningful degree after age 13.[2]

And this, in my humble opinion, is his most significant finding:

> Studies pointed out that most Christian churches evaluate success in terms of program attendance, child satisfaction, and parental satisfaction, but do little to examine the individual spiritual advancement. *However, the ministries having the greatest success at seeing young people emerge into mature Christians, rather than contented church goers, are those that facilitate a parent-church partnership focused on instilling specific spiritual beliefs and practices in a child's life from a very early age.* Sadly, less than one out of every five churches has produced such a ministry.[3]
>
> —EMPHASIS ADDED

Parents in the New Millennium

Did you know that research has shown that 85 percent of all parents believe they have the primary responsibility for teaching their children about religious beliefs and spiritual matters. Add to that a whopping "96 percent of all parents…contend that they have the primary responsibility for teaching their children values. Related research, however, revealed that a majority of parents do not spend any time during a typical week discussing religious matters or studying religious materials with their children."[4]

According the Barna Research Group, "Parents typically have no plan for the spiritual development of their children, do not consider it a priority, have little or no training in how to nurture a child's faith, have no related standards or goals that they are seeking to satisfy, and experience no accountability for their efforts. *The very people who claim responsibility for the spiritual growth of their children are doing little about it beyond dropping their kids off at church*" (emphasis added).[5]

Wow! If this is true, then the implications of these findings are enormous for the church here in America and ultimately our ability to reach and affect the world we live in. What about you? What about your home? Do these findings describe you? If the answer is yes, you are obviously not alone. And you are also not a terrible parent.

If this or any part of this sounds remotely familiar, then this book was written specifically for you. It contains a message I believe God gave me to give to you. As you read this book, I truly believe that in God's sovereignty, He has appointed this as a time of reflection and admonition for you and for your family. So dig in, get out a highlighter or a marker, and let the journey begin. The destination is definitely worthy of your time, attention, and devotion. I can promise you that.

EYES TO SEE WHAT IS TRUE

In a service at my home church, our pastor, Jentezen Franklin, relayed a story to us that truly illustrates the "starting place" for the journey you are about to take. He speaks at different places across the country nearly every week. This has required him to fly almost weekly. Because of so many trips, there are occasions when the copilot is not able to come, which my pastor loves because when the copilot does not travel with them, he is allowed to sit in the copilot's seat.

He told us that flying into a city at night in search of the airport landing area or runway can be extremely difficult for an untrained eye. In fact, the pilot has a button he is able to push that causes the runway lights to flash on and off to make it easier to spot. My pastor says that even then he cannot, with his untrained eye, spot the runways on many occasions, but the pilot, with his trained eye, can pick out the runway with ease.

Why is that? Is it because his eyes are better? Is it because he knows the area better? Is it because he has learned some special navigational technique that enables him to mechanically locate the runway? No. The reason the pilot is able to spot the airport and the runway with ease and accuracy is because his eyes have been trained to see the lights. Even more importantly, he has been trained to distinguish the runway lights from the thousands of other lights in the city.

That, in a nutshell, is what this book is designed to do. It is designed to help you see what is true about your child, as well as to enable you to parent with discernment, wisdom, and courage. Like the lights of the city, the world has a thousand messages it wants you to hear, a million voices vying for your attention, and hundreds of philosophies on how to best rear your children. My goal is to help you see beneath the surface and hear amidst the deafening cry of the world that still, small voice and to help you take courageous steps of faith. Walk this path with me over the next few weeks and get all the way in, and, as the book's title denotes, take the steps necessary to parent at the next level.

SECTION I

THE AWAKENING

For our light and momentary troubles are achieving for us an eternal glory that far outweighs them all. So we fix our eyes not on what is seen, *but on what is unseen. For what is seen is temporary, but what is unseen is eternal.*

2 CORINTHIANS 4:17–18, EMPHASIS ADDED

chapter 1

ADMIT THERE IS A PROBLEM

So what good does it do us to build strong families if they
don't know the Creator of families?[1]

—DR. JAMES DOBSON

SEVERAL YEARS AGO, we were blessed to be able to move into a beautiful two-story home with four bedrooms, two and a half baths,
and a bonus room that we used as a toy room. It was the American
dream. At the time, our children were ages five, three, and one. It was
incredible. But wait, it gets better! Not only did we live at the end of the
street, but the house was also in a cul-de-sac with a park that began where
the cul-de-sac ended.

On top of all this was the additional room off the living room that we
converted into a TV/family room, complete with a fireplace and slider that
led to a private patio. This was *my* room, and I was in heaven! I had my
special chair, my remote control, and my beautiful, full-sized Technicolor,
picture-in-a-picture television. I had it all!

But the greatest blessing of all, or so I thought, was that there were about
ten to twelve other children in the neighborhood, all about the same age as
my girls (and a few just a little bit older). It was great! Our children played
outside all of the time and had a blast. They were healthy, active, social, and

loving life. Not only did our children get to be outside playing for hours on end, but they were also developing friendships with these children that has lasted several years after my work moved us away.

However, something happened to us over the eighteen months we were there that was akin to the frog in the boiling water story. At the time, I was very involved in being a school administrator, coaching, and finishing my doctoral work. This was all in addition to our weekly involvement at our church. While I have never been a very private person or one who needs privacy and quiet times alone, I never protested to the extra time undisturbed in *my room* during those months, and I would spend hours in my special room, watching television or reading.

Somewhere around month fourteen or fifteen of living in this house I started becoming more and more conscious of the amount of time that the kids were out playing with their friends. They could literally play for hours on end, within full view of the house, safe and secure. But what I began to sense in my spirit was a drifting away, a subtle separation from my own children.

This did not alarm me too much at first, and I chalked most of it up to a normal childhood. But what really began to catch my attention was some of the statements my girls were making and the music they were listening to. Even more alarming to me was the ability of my children to sing, word for word, so many of these songs.

Then it hit me. We were losing our kids. There was no big dramatic event, argument, or confrontation, just a simple, very subtle change in the spirit and affections my children were beginning to embrace. While at the same time, Daddy was becoming less and less significant and far less relevant in their little world.

Now, I want to be very clear about something. Our neighbors were wonderful people. They were all very caring parents who dedicated their time and resources to raising "good kids." But it was also very true that most were not Christians, and that some did not share our worldview. Did they know we were Christians? Yes. Were we able to reach some for Christ? Praise God, yes! But were we losing our kids? Absolutely. I remember thinking that if I could feel that way when my children were six, four, and two, what must it be like for a parent of a teenager to make such a discovery?

I knew then that it was time to engage. We began the painful process of having those tough conversations with my children, and we began to reshape their days and nights. Mostly, we began to pay attention. It is amazing the things we will see and hear if we just pay attention. It is so much easier to let them do their thing while we do ours, but in the overall scheme of things, we have to pay attention. We began to listen to the lyrics of the music they were listening to. We began to listen in on some of their conversations, and then we began to have input into their day, during the day—then again when we had their full attention during those precious minutes tucking them in at the end of their day.

It was a tough process because my children truly loved their friends. That pull of the world was a constant presence. Yes, they would invite and take their friends to church on many occasions, and they were never far from our own front door, yet there was still the constant pull of the world with all of its subtle attractions and relationships.

While I was processing what the Lord was showing me through all of this at home, at work I was dealing, every day, with parents of high schoolers who were at a loss for how to get their kids back. I was the dean of students at the local high school, and most of my day was spent with students and families who were struggling. It was my job to deal with the many discipline situations that occurred daily in a high school with more than 2,100 students. While most were minor violations, there were plenty of major situations— broken kids, frustrated parents, and divided homes. Almost every day, I was a witness to what the experts refer to as "disconnect."

More often than not, it was readily apparent that the ones who had disconnected along the way were the adults—not the kids. The kids were just the ones struggling with the life decisions the parents had made and with finding someone, someplace, or something to "connect" to other than them.

I also need to point out that these were not the only students I dealt with. In fact, the students with disciplinary issues were only a small percentage of the overall population of the school. Most of the students in this school were doing extremely well with the "good kid" stuff. In fact, most of the parents at the school were definitely parenting at the next level, but it was in the physical realm. They went the extra mile every day, were on top of nearly everything, and had great kids, but something was still missing. It was during this time in my life, with all its varied experiences, that the Lord impressed upon me the calling to write this book.

He began to show me that while we can do everything above and beyond for our children in the physical realm, and they can excel and succeed, the most important part of their development—and ours—begins in the heart. All through the Bible, we are told again and again that it is the heart of man that matters most. It is the heart where Christ wants to be enthroned, not the mind, not the outward behaviors, and not in accomplishments. It's interesting that He would choose the thing that lies deepest beneath the surface to house that which is truest of each of us. It's strange that it would be something we cannot see with human eyes that would determine our eternal destiny, but that is what He has ordained to be true.

THE AGE-OLD DECEPTION

While flipping through the channels late one night, I stopped to watch an interesting scenario unfold on the nature channel. It was a piece about the hunting habits of lions and how they work together to secure their prey. The story explained that when lions get too old to hunt, they work themselves upwind of their prey and wait for the younger lions to hide downwind from the prey. When the stage is set, the old lions begin to make their move.

Instead of trying to chase down their prey, the older and wiser lions simply begin to roar loudly and slowly move toward the prey. What is really amazing though is to watch the prey because their senses tell them to run away from the roar, but their instincts tell them something is not quite right here. In fact, the secret to escape in this situation is to not trust their senses and to instead run in the direction of the roar. The prey who were motivated by basic reactions ran straight to their death. As uncanny as that may seem, the ones who survived were the ones who did not fall for the schemes of the older lions and instead ran right through the falsely intimidating roar of the toothless predator, trusting their instincts rather than their circumstances.

What an incredible analogy for the challenge our children will face in the years ahead. The world will roar, telling them which way to go. Satan will tempt them when they are at their weakest, and their peers will pull them in every direction, many times away from what they instinctively know is right.

Beth Moore, one of the most gifted and anointed speakers and authors of our modern era, speaks clearly to the attack the church is under. In one of her works *When Godly People Do Ungodly Things*, she goes to great lengths to convey not only the truth and the scriptural perspective regarding this war we face but also the urgency of the message as well. She says:

> In the midst of the winds of evil currently blowing in our world today, Christians will do well to remember that the Evil One still lurks, waiting to seduce those who belong to the Lord, seeking to destroy the testimony of their walk with God.
>
> It is reported in the headlines, confessed in the pulpits, and hidden in the pews in the churches around the world. The seduction of God's people by the deceiver is a tale as old as the garden, but we are always surprised when it happens. We must realize that Satan is a lion on the prowl and we are his prey.[2]

Beth speaks and pleads with the church as one who has seen the hurt and devastation in the lives of flesh-and-blood people who have succumbed to the ploys of the great deceiver. She concludes:

We, Christ's church, are in desperate need of developing His heart and mind in issues like these.[3]

CORRECTIVE MEASURES—GENERATION LAST

So much has been written in the past fifteen to twenty years about parenting techniques and strategies. In fact, not since the days of Dr. Spock has so much been written about how to produce "well-behaved" children. Perhaps the greatest source of this material has come largely from the Christian community. One Christian leader in particular, Dr. James Dobson, founder of Focus on the Family, came on the scene in the late 1970s armed with a divine message from above in the form of a breakthrough book called *Dare to Discipline*. It went through the roof in sales as a hungry nation of parents desperately searched for ways to take back their families from a society gone mad with self-indulgence and excess. Since that time there have been numerous church and parachurch organizations that have stepped up to the plate and entered the war on behalf of the family.

When Focus on the Family came on the scene, the nation had just come through one of the most morally turbulent twenty-year periods in our two-hundred-year history. Notably in 1968 *TIME* magazine referred to this period as "a knife blade that severed the past from the future."[4] One by one, we watched in terror as the leaders of the free world were gunned down in cold blood, and we looked on in horror at the steady stream of body bags that were displayed on our television sets night after night as they arrived from the battlefields of Vietnam.

It was during this turbulent time that one famous outspoken atheist, John Lennon, of Beatles fame, was quoted saying:

Christianity will go. It will vanish and shrink. I needn't argue about that: I'm right, and I will be proved right. We're more popular than Jesus now…Jesus was all right, but his disciples were thick and ordinary.[5]

Chuck Colson, in his book *The Problem of Evil*, says this of that tumultuous time:

> Make no mistake. The sixties were not just an era of long hair and bell-bottoms. It was an intellectual and cultural upheaval that marked the end of modernity's optimism and introduced the worldview of despair on a broad level. Ideas concocted in the rarefied domain of academia filtered down to shape an entire generation of young people. They, in turn, have brought those ideas to their logical conclusion in postmodernism, *with its suspicion of the very notions of reason and objective truth.*[6]
>
> —EMPHASIS ADDED

And with that, the gauntlet had been thrown down and the war for the minds of the next generation and the offspring they would spawn was in full array.

Meanwhile, the church was struggling to reach a nation of believers who were in search of practical ways to live out their faith. The most tragic of all situations was taking place in the homes of our nation and, in particular, the Christian homes. Christian parents were losing control of their children at an alarming rate. Parental discipline and correction was suddenly seen as archaic, and anything that stood in the way of absolute freedom was seen as a moral evil.

It is curious to note, but the word *crisis*, when written in Chinese, is composed of two characters. One character represents danger, *but the other represents opportunity.* Enter God's movement for such a time as this. Dr. James Dobson and Focus on the Family courageously stepped in to help the nation's churches stand in the gap for parents in the form of teaching and information that would help right a sinking ship, specifically in the area of child development and basic child-rearing strategies. His flagship book *Dare to Discipline* turned out to be the beginning of one of the most effective family ministries, perhaps in the history of the modern church, as the Focus on the Family organization was birthed.

The impact was immediate and lasting as thousands upon thousands of letters and phone calls to the Focus on the Family headquarters can attest. I can remember listening weekly to the Focus on the Family broadcasts with great interest and excitement, even as a young single adult, as God spoke to me personally each and every week through this humble servant of God.

Many struggling Christian parents began unashamedly taking back their families and restoring order to their homes, while already strong homes gained insight, encouragement, and affirmation in a world that was offering just the opposite. God had a message for the Christian families of this nation, and Focus on the Family, along with other notable Christian leaders, church family ministries, and parachurch organizations, stood on a hill and proclaimed that message with courage and confidence...for a season.

But now we are seeing a new breed of problems facing our families. It is not as simple as telling our children not to fight at recess. Our children are being attacked from all sides—the media, the agenda of secular humanist teachers and professors, the Internet, music, and so much more. In this next chapter, I will give a clear description of what we are now facing. This kind of problem identification is key to making a lasting difference in the lives of our children and the generations to come.

chapter 2

THE PROBLEM DEFINED

Christianity, if false, is of no importance, and if true, of
infinite importance. The only thing it cannot be is moderately
important.[1]

— C. S. LEWIS

As mentioned in the introduction, there has been a tremendous
effort on the part of the church and parachurch organizations in the
United States to come alongside parents to assist them, strengthen
them, encourage them, and equip them for the awesome task that they are
charged with—parenting the children God has placed in their care.

The effects of these efforts have been far reaching and extremely effective
in helping parents raise well-mannered, respectful, well-behaved children
who do well in school, excel in extracurricular school and church activities,
and possess good moral character and decision-making skills. These efforts
yield good, productive citizens who replicate this model in their own child-
rearing practices when it becomes their turn to parent.

"What's so bad about that?" you might ask. My response is that there is
nothing "so bad about that." But if we are to reach our children for Christ in
the days that lie ahead, *we must do more*. We must go to the next level in our
parenting practices and strategies, thus the title for this book. But rather than
considering this as an added set of duties and responsibilities, I am going to do
everything I can in the pages that follow to convince you that understanding

and implementing next-level parenting practices and strategies is not what we have to add to anything, but rather it is the place we must *begin*.

THE MYTH: GOOD KID = NO PROBLEM

The focus for many Christian parents—and churches, for that matter—has been on outward behaviors and physical outcomes. Herein is the problem. The emphasis cannot only be placed on raising "good" kids. Just ask anyone what a good kid looks like and they will tell you:

- Good manners

- Good morals

- Well behaved

- Respectful of authority, especially teachers

- Responsible

- Shows us love

- Good and positive attitude

- Does well in school

- Cares about and helps serve others

- Good work ethic

- Always does his or her best

- Good loser and winner

- Sympathizes to others

- Contributes to the home (i.e., chores, other responsibilities)

- Productive citizen

Who wouldn't want a child that embodied these qualities? In fact, this child probably does not even exist. But if he or she did, in the eyes of most of us, any combination of these qualities makes up a great kid. However, as we proceed through this book, I hope to point out that while there is nothing wrong with what is listed above, that list absent a profound, walking, talking, loving relationship with Jesus Christ is of little value. These character traits do not guarantee that what matters most—a relationship with Christ—has been established and taken root. Scripture says it like this: "What good is it for a man to gain the whole world, yet forfeit his soul?" (Mark 8:36).

Children are intelligent beings. They have learned a very simple yet tragic lesson about their parents, their teachers, and sadly their church. This costly lesson is that if they simply act the way we want them to act, we will leave them alone. They have learned to "stay off the radar," so to speak. This is exactly what is happening to our children during the years when they need us the most—we are leaving them alone. All the while, Satan and the forces of darkness are vying for their interests at an unprecedented level of intensity. The cry of every troubled teen is, "Leave me alone!" And far too many times, we accommodate that request.

Consider this true story from the April 30, 2006, edition of the *Pittsburgh Tribune Review*: Jamie Greene was a happy, well-behaved teenager from a good middle-class home. She was an A student with perfect attendance. She wanted to be a nurse and loved to ride horses. Shortly after her eighteenth birthday, between her junior and senior years at Norwin High School, Greene tried heroin and quickly became addicted. Three years later, she was dead of an overdose. "From the first day she snorted heroin, it robbed her of her life. It took a high-spirited, very pretty, outgoing, polite young woman and turned her into a dishrag," said Greene's mother, Diane Shields of North Huntingdon. "It robbed her brain from ever being normal again. It took her skin and turned it into scars. It turned her into a criminal. Spirituality, it robbed her of that."[2]

Alfie Kohn is a very popular author and speaker on topics related to education and schooling. His breakthrough article, "How Not to Teach Values," features a quote from John Holt that speaks well to this topic:

Teachers and schools tend to mistake good behavior for good character. What they prize is docility, suggestibility; the child who will do what he is told; or even better, the child who will do what is wanted without even having to be told. They value most in children what children least value in themselves. Small wonder that their effort to build character is such a failure; they don't know it when they see it.[3]

THE INVISIBLE FORK IN THE ROAD

I want to make one thing clear. I in no way want to imply that this tragic occurrence is a deliberate act of neglect or inactivity on the part of parents. On the contrary, we are working harder and longer than we ever have to give them everything we never had. But we do this while our children spend afternoons at their friend's house, or evenings retreating for a few hours here and there to the place behind the closed door we call their room, or long lazy days playing innocently for hours with the neighborhood kids.

Each of these activities, while seeming innocent in and of themselves, add up to hours, days, then weeks and years. The tragic result is that systematically, over time, we are losing our children to that familiar enemy—the world. In fact, what we awake to find is that our children have forged relationships with everyone but us. Then, amazingly, we act surprised when our children's views resemble the world they grew up in a whole lot more than the set of values we had hoped they would learn an hour or two a day with us, plus an hour a week in Sunday school or youth group. We make the tragic mistake of assuming that because they live up to our standards and are good people, they will make our God their God and will follow our God in the same ways they have since they were children. But in far too many Christian homes across this country, it simply did not take.

So it must be our quest, our decided purpose, to know the hearts of our children. It must be our highest goal to see Christ enthroned there. It is our most important job, in my estimation, to continually teach and prepare that heart with the goal of it being as open and as fertile as possible for all God would put there.

What has God shown me regarding this most noble of causes? What have I learned? I have learned, through study, observation, and experience, that I cannot accomplish this sitting in the TV room while my children spend hours, days, and weeks in the company of the world. I have learned that the great deceiver, Satan, wants nothing more than to lull me into that place of disaster called complacency. I have learned that I must answer the bell—give all that I have, and parent at the next level. And I have seen with my own eyes the consequences of those, including myself, who would choose to do otherwise.

chapter 3

THE MESSAGE OF
NEXT LEVEL PARENTING

A lie cannot live.[1]

—Martin Luther King Jr.

This is because our choices are shaped by what we believe is real and true, right and wrong, or good and beautiful. In short, our choices are shaped by…our "worldview."[2]

—Charles Colson

A FEW YEARS AGO I had the privilege of attending a conference hosted by Pastor Chuck Smith at the Anaheim Convention Center in Anaheim, California. Pastor Chuck, as he is affectionately referred to by his congregation, is the pastor and founder of the Calvary Chapel churches that have sprung up all across America and the world. In his address to the leaders present that night, he spoke as a voice of warning.

One thing he said struck me as both prophetic and profound. He began his message by stating, "There are storms on the horizon for God's church here in the U.S. and across the world." He then went on to detail the assault that was already underway as well as the ones on the horizon. Chuck was right. God used him that night to warn the church through the many leaders from different denominations gathered there. He told them that they needed to prepare for battle, a battle perhaps whose assault on the church would be greater than ever before. How could he know then about September 11, the priest scandals that the Catholic church would have to endure, the presidential elections of 2000, 2004, and 2008, the battle regarding the Ten Commandments, the advancement of the homosexual agenda, the key Supreme Court decisions, financial bailouts, the hundreds of evangelical churches nationwide that would soon close their doors, or any number of other major events that have occurred in the church since that time? How could he know? *He knew because God showed him.* He knew because he was a student of the times and of the Word. He knew because of his discerning heart and his sensitivity to the moving of the spirit of God—as well as the movement of the deceiver.

In the years since, I have watched this attack take place both here in the United States and abroad at unprecedented levels, as I am sure you have. What has struck me to the core these last few years is the startling realization that the family is the first point of attack in this war. The family is literally under siege. You must understand that it is our children who are the trophy Satan seeks to have as his own. They are the generation that all eyes are on as all eternity looks on.

In Africa alone, there is an entire generation presently that will grow up absent any formal family structure, as parents are succumbing by the millions to the deadly disease AIDS. Consider this: the AIDS epidemic has left more than thirteen million children with neither father nor mother.[3]

How about here at home in the United States? Consider that each day in America:

- Four children are killed by abuse or neglect.

- Five children or teens commit suicide (that's more than eighteen hundred per year).

- One hundred fifty-five children are arrested for violent crimes.

- Almost three hundred are arrested for drug crimes.

- More than eleven hundred babies are born to teenage mothers.

- Almost twenty-five hundred high school students drop out.[4]

The reality is this: just as the physical wars are at an advanced level in other countries, the spiritual wars here in America—the so-called Christian nation—are just as advanced, with equally devastating eternal implications.

RELIGION IN THE NEW MILLENNIUM

In an article titled "Spiritual Progress Hard to Find in 2003," George Barna details the findings of his study, analyzing more than ten thousand personal interviews nationwide. Contradictions and confusion permeate the spiritual condition of the nation. Some notable findings of the study are as follows:

- Religious faith is very important in their own life to 84 percent of respondents.

- Personal religious faith is consistently growing deeper for 70 percent of respondents.

- Eighty-four percent claim to be Christians.

- Sixty percent say they believe the Bible is totally accurate in all that it teaches.

- Seventy-five percent say they are absolutely or somewhat committed to Christianity.[5]

The same people say that the following behaviors and lifestyles are "morally acceptable":

- Cohabitation—60 percent

- Gambling—61 percent

- Adultery—42 percent

- Sexual relations between homosexuals—30 percent

- Abortion—45 percent (In the United States, nearly 45 million babies have been sacrificed since the *Roe v. Wade* decision in 1973.)[6]

- Pornography—38 percent

- Use of profanity—36 percent[7]

I once conducted research and took a look at the lyrics of the top ten songs in the United States for the week ending November 29, 2003.[8] All across this country, our preteens, teens, and young adults listen to these songs. In my research I found more than 115 instances where profanity was used, many times extreme use. I also found more than 65 derogatory titles and names used to refer to females, and more than 65 references to overt sexual (not romantic) acts. This was in addition to the numerous references made to violent acts of aggression and hatred.

As I do Next Level Parenting conferences, I will usually check the latest top ten singles for the United States to give a snapshot of what our young people consider "entertainment" and what is allowed to invade the minds of so many impressionable young hearts and souls. Additionally, in an ad by the Parents and Grandparents Alliance in the *Kansas City Star*, the National Education Association (NEA) research findings are quoted saying, "Many of the thousands of teen suicides each year are linked to music lyrics!"[9]

While 84 percent of those surveyed in the aforementioned Barna survey claimed to be Christians, the following is profound:

- Just 38 percent have confessed their sins and accepted Christ as their Savior.

- Ninety-nine percent claim they will not go to hell after they die.

- The vast majority do not believe in the existence of Satan or hell.[10]

This is our Father's world, but it is a world that is going its own way, resulting in a world where the darkness—*spiritual darkness*—is very great. Not to mention the fact that the American statistics given above are a reflection of what people say. What they do, how they live, and how they define God make all the difference in the world as to how one would weigh these responses.

A SAFE HAVEN?

Let me bring it closer to home for a moment. Consider this: according to the experts, Christian and secular alike, the church in America is not the safe haven we would hope it would be, as the statistics for many of the ills of society are no different than those for the unsaved world.

Dr. Henry Blackaby, coauthor of the best-selling book and workbook *Experiencing God*, spoke on May 22, 1999, to a conference of pastors at the Billy Graham Training Center at the Cove in Ashville, North Carolina. After he was finished speaking, he was asked this question by one of the conference attendees: "What do you see as the future for the United States?" Dr. Blackaby replied:

> If you put the US up against the Scriptures, we're in trouble. I think we're very close to the judgment of God. The problem of America is not the unbelieving world. The problem of America is the people of God. You see, right now, there are just as many divorces in the churches as outside the churches. There are just as many abortions inside the churches as outside the churches. There's only a one percent difference in gambling inside the churches as outside the churches. George Barna did a survey of 152 separate items comparing the lost world and the churches, and he said there is virtually no difference between the two. So we have brokenness in the churches [and] no

reconciliation. It's God's people who hold the destiny of America. Don't fuss at the world. It's acting just like its nature. We've got to be salt and light again. We've got to have an observable difference.[11]

The exact findings of the Barna studies referred to by Blackaby show that "33 percent of all born again individuals who have been married have gone through a divorce, which is statistically identical to the 34 percent incidence among non–born-again adults."[12] But even more significant is the fact that "more than 90 percent of the born-again adults who have been divorced experienced that divorce after they accepted Christ, not before."[13]

In the pages of this book, I will walk you through a progression that begins with acknowledging there is a problem and ends with the glorious victory that is yours for the taking. The message of this book is summed up below, and each point listed will be covered during the course of this journey.

NEXT-LEVEL PARENTING OVERVIEW

Take a minute to look over this list while knowing that the power to parent at the next level is very much within your grasp. Take a look at the list below, summon the courage to take the first steps, and then begin your journey, knowing that there is an incredible message from God written directly to you for your purposes in your generation. As you read this, pray for clarity and truth, then get all the way in—one day at a time.

- You must admit that there is a problem.

- You must understand the source and nature of the problem.

- You must understand the historical context and the spiritual and scriptural significance of what is happening.

- You must arm yourself with the truth and begin to parent at the next level by knowing your children, teaching them, telling them, and preparing them for the journey ahead.

- You must discover that the most important truth to internalize or accept is that there are two worldviews: Christian and secular. There is only good and evil in this world, with very little in between.

- You must also grasp the concepts associated with darkness and light.

- You must learn to see with your Father's eyes and to discern what is true.

- You must commit, as a parent, to get all the way in and grow deep.

- You must realize that at the center of everything we will ever strive to accomplish lies one unchangeable factor—ME.

- You must declare you intentions after coming to grips with this awesome concept and the blessings that come from a life where there is spiritual depth. Or, you must also face the tragic ramifications of a life that refuses to grow.

- You must see that God has a plan, not just a generic plan, but rather a plan specifically designed for you, as well as a plan and a purpose for your child. You must see that we are truly called to be a people of joy, with children of hope, who can and do live lives that give testimony to the victory that has already been won. You must "go out with joy, and be led forth with peace" (Isa. 55:12, NAS).

That, in short, is the message I want to impress upon your heart throughout this book. We cannot simply go through the motions. We must understand that a war is raging all around us. It is a war you signed up for when you declared yourself a Christian and a war that only intensified the day you took on one of the most treasured titles given by God—Mommy or Daddy.

But this is a war that Scripture tells us is ours for the winning, and it is not a war we wage alone, for He has promised that He will go with us into battle and that He will defend us, protect us, and deliver us at every turn. Many children have already been taken hostage.

What will you do? Will you fight for your child? Will you lay down your life for your family? Will you stand in the gap? *Wake up and slumber no more, you who call yourselves Christian parents*, as your appointed time of battle is at hand, and the eternal souls of your children are at stake.

chapter 4

STATE OF THE CHRISTIAN
FAMILY ADDRESS

> We are at war. The world in which we live is a combat zone,
> a violent clash of kingdoms, a bitter struggle unto the death.
> You were born into a world at war, and you will live out all
> your days in the midst of the great battle, involving all the
> forces of heaven and hell and played out here on earth.[1]
>
> —JOHN ELDREDGE

IN APRIL OF 1998, I was driving through Orange County, California,
to drop off a paper for a class in my doctoral program. I can still
remember it vividly. On the way to the drop-off center, I listened
intently to the radio program *Focus on the Family* as Dr. Dobson interviewed
a man by the name of Jim Taylor. They were discussing a booklet published
annually by the Young America's Foundation called *Comedy and Tragedy*. This,
by the way, is updated every year and is a must-read for parents of prospec-
tive college students who are trying to decide which college or university is
the best fit. The title of the two-day series on *Focus on the Family* was Higher
Education: What You Learn Could Hurt You. The broadcast was essentially a collection of absolute horror stories of Christian parents who were
losing their children to the world through the ungodly influences of liberal
teachings, professors, and peers they encountered on college campuses.[2] The
booklet was and is a yearly collection of evidence designed to expose what is
going on and being taught on college campuses all across America.

The letters Dr. Dobson read that day from parents were filled with sadness and brokenness. These were parents who thought they did all the right things. The stories went something like this:

> Johnny comes from an evangelical family, and he went to church nearly every Sunday since he was born. He did well in Awana as a child and was even a part of his youth group activity leadership team. His parents saw to it that he did well in school. He seemed to have nice friends and was very respectful to authority. Johnny wasn't perfect, mind you, but he was a good boy and was considered by all who knew him as a fine Christian young man. So you can imagine the utter shock when Johnny came home after his sophomore year in college and announced that he is now a homosexual and has no tolerance for that narrow-minded, bigoted, ancient Christian dogma that he was once so naïve to follow.

> Cindy was the class valedictorian and captain of her high school cross-country team. She never had behavior problems growing up, and she went to church with her parents every week. She had quite a bit of freedom when in high school, yes, but she was always home by her curfew and did everything she was asked to do around the house. Sure, there wasn't a lot of "talk" that went on with Mom and Dad during the teenage years, but she was a teenager. So it just seemed normal that she would spend more time with her friends than she did with her family. Cindy went to a top Ivy League school, and everything seemed to be going great. Then her parents got the phone call form Cindy saying she wouldn't be coming home that summer and that she would be moving off campus to live with her boyfriend in an apartment near campus. Her parents cry out to the Lord and say, "How can this be?"

These stories have become a daily occurrence in many Christian homes all across this nation. The stories also illustrate the point that there are literally thousands of young people who are graduating from high school, leaving our nests, and walking away from church and the Christian heritage they were brought up under, in search of something they will never find outside the body of Christ—their *purpose*, their true *identity*, and *truth*.

At a recent conference, a representative from the Barna Research Institute told us that research now shows that 80 percent of people who regularly attended church in their teens will leave the church by age twenty-nine.[3]

Additionally, a recent *Focus on the Family* broadcast revealed that 61 percent of high school seniors who had taken a pledge of abstinence as a senior broke that pledge in college.[4]

Where did we lose them? Where did we go wrong? Were these kids ever truly saved? Was it all for naught? Is it too late? You may be asking, "Can this happen to my child? What can I do as a parent right now to help prevent this from happening to my child? How can we as a church stand in the gap and stop this terrible exodus, this tragic loss of life and hope?" These are profound questions in need of practical answers.

HOPE AND A PLAN

Consider this: it is true that a growing body of research shows that people in the eighteen to twenty-nine age group are walking out the doors of churches at record pace, many never to return. But there is also recent findings that point toward hope and a plan. George Barna states:

> Research underscores the importance of families, not churches, taking the lead in the spiritual development of children. In situations where children became mature Christians we usually found a symbiotic partnership between their parents and the church. The church encouraged parents to prioritize the spiritual development of their children and worked hard to equip them for that challenge. Parents, for their part, raised their children in the context of a faith-based community that provided security, belonging, spiritual

and moral education, and accountability. Neither the church nor the parents could have done it alone.[5]

I recently came across an extremely important article in the *USA Today* newspaper. *USA Today*, not exactly known for its conservative slant or its friendliness to the church, actually reported on the results of a study on parenting. The title of the article (buried in section D, page 9) was "Do Evangelical Protestant Fathers Really Know Best?" The findings of this study, conducted by University of Virginia sociologist W. Bradford Wilcox, found that *indeed they do . . . significantly.* Says Wilcox, "Evangelical Protestant dads came out on top compared with every religious group in the US. The study included different religious groups including Catholics and Protestant denominations, Jews, Muslims, as well as fathers with no religious background affiliations." The study concluded the following:

> Evangelical Protestant men are more likely to expect their school-age children to tell them where they are at all times and more likely to hug and be affectionate toward their kids than religiously unaffiliated men. They also spend more time in youth activities with their kids.[6]

And here is the kicker, says Wilcox:

> Religious congregations give young families social support and enforce certain *norms* about what it means to be a good father.[7]

There is hope. There absolutely is hope, and there is a plan. Nothing surprises God—not the ills of society, not the plight of the church, and not the daily comings and goings in your home. Better still, your love for your child does not begin to compare with *His* love for your child. He has a plan, and you are right in the center of that plan. So, I challenge you right now, wherever you are, to take your eyes off your circumstances and place them on Him.

SECTION II

KNOW YOUR CHILD—ASK THE RIGHT QUESTIONS

A child miseducated is a child lost.[1]

JOHN F. KENNEDY

chapter 5

CAUSE AND EFFECT

By wisdom a house is built, and *through understanding it is established*; through knowledge its rooms are filled with rare and beautiful treasures.

—PROVERBS 24:3–4, EMPHASIS ADDED

CROCKETT JR HIGH SCHOOL
LIBRARY
ODESSA, TEXAS

I N THE LAST section, we identified a very real problem aimed at destroying our children and our families. The next obvious question would be, Can this happen to my family? The primary issue that every parent has to examine is whether the seeds, the spiritual values we have endeavored to instill, have taken root or have instead just fallen on unfertile soil, only to be blown away with the winds of time.

How will you know? I believe the answer is found in the scripture given above. How will you know? By God giving you *wisdom, understanding, and knowledge.* This section of the book is committed to that task.

SAND AND STONE

Let me ask you a few fundamental questions. What will your child need when things go wrong? What will your child need when they have tremendous success? What will your child need when their beliefs are challenged? On the following page I have listed examples of real-life situations, most of which will be experienced by every human at some time or another. This means your child…and mine.

Life experiences

- Death of a close friend or family member

- Birth of a newborn baby

- Failure

- Success

- Unreasonably high expectations

- Criticism

- Broken relationship

- Marriage

- Lost job

- Moral failure

- Spiritual mountaintop

- Sickness or injury

- Financial struggles

- Great wealth

- Lust

- Temptation

- University professor or teacher that challenges core Christian beliefs

What will they need when these things occur? When I ask this question at conferences, there is always an awkward silence for a moment as parents are confronted with having to answer a question regarding topics we tend to avoid. Yet when I pose the question, all agree that most of their children will encounter most of the things on the list, and all will encounter at least a few of the items.

What will they need? When the storms of life are howling, what will they need? When the very ground they stand on is shaken, what will they need? When their beliefs are challenged and they do not have all the answers, what will they need? When their hormones are raging and their lusts are stirred, what will they need?

I believe that in all of these situations they will need the following:

1. An eternal perspective—the long view. The ability to see what God sees with eternity as the backdrop

2. A Christian worldview—His eyes, His ears, His heart

3. A place to call home—family, godly friends, their church family

4. Godly character and integrity—inner strength, endurance, and conviction

5. Truth—discernment, facts, knowledge, and wisdom

6. Hope—trusting that God has a plan and a purpose for their lives that supersedes present circumstances

FAITH WITH ROOTS

Wouldn't you agree that our children need to embrace the themes listed above? But how do you get them there? Or maybe the better question would be, What is keeping these essentials from taking root in my child? Where are the roadblocks?

Three major causes for unbelief

To answer this question, you must go deeper and examine the root issues involved. As I have researched, observed, and examined this "taking root" issue, I have come to believe that there are three major causes for seeds not taking root, and these causes must be addressed:

1. The child does not believe that God is real.

2. For those who believe He is real, they have yet to truly stand in His presence, resulting in "head faith" only.

3. The world has become an incredibly attractive place.

How do you address these issues? First, you must ask the right questions. Second, you must be willing to have some very courageous conversations. What is true for your child? Do you know? While these spiritual deterrents may sound simple and straightforward, upon deeper examination I think you will find each of these three items to be incredibly revealing and profound. Let's look at each of these statements a little more in depth. But I must warn you, the path can only be traversed by way of honest, courageous conversations with your child. And remember, what is at stake, once again, is the following:

1. An eternal perspective

2. A Christian worldview

3. A place to call home

4. Godly character and integrity

5. Truth

6. Hope

As you move through the next set of chapters, be bold in your approach, knowing all of heaven stands with you in the greatest battle of our lifetime— the battle for the very souls of our children.

chapter 6

CAUSE FOR UNBELIEF (PART 1): IS GOD REAL?

I gave in, and admitted that God was God...I believe in Christianity as I believe that the sun has risen; not only because I see it, but because by it I see everything else.[1]

—C. S. LEWIS

I
F A CHILD truly believes that God is real and that Jesus Christ is the Son of God, what should that look like in everyday life? While we will examine the causes that led a generation of believers down the path toward disbelief, for our purposes here and now, we must step back and ask this basic, rudimentary question: *does your child fear God?*

The Bible says in Proverbs 1:7, "The fear of the LORD is the *beginning* of knowledge, but fools despise wisdom and discipline" (emphasis added).

Does your child fear God? This issue of fear does not mean to be afraid or in constant worry, but rather it does your child good to consider what the Lord thinks about his or her thoughts, deeds, or actions. When weighing what God thinks, it should influence decisions they make. Is your child concerned about consequences and the approval of a being as powerful and all-knowing as God? Tough questions, but I believe, when researched, you will find them to be incredibly revealing.

LOOKING BENEATH THE SURFACE

Here are some simple but compelling questions for you to consider as you endeavor to truly know your child:

1. Does your child think that there really is a divine being out there who knows their thoughts, sees their deeds, and judges their actions?

2. Do they know the One who loves them deeply, who hears them when they speak to Him, and who can truly be a friend that is closer than a brother?

3. Do they believe with all of their heart that they were created for a purpose and that God has a plan for their life that is so much more powerful and awesome than any plan or dream they can conceive?

These are all very profound questions that I am asking you to discern about your child, but if in doubt about any or all, try to find out what your child thinks about the Word of God.

1. Does your child understand that this book contains truth so powerful that history was actually foretold hundreds of years in advance, and that there are parts of the Bible that speak to events that are occurring even during our lifetime?

2. Do they believe that the words contained in the Bible are actually God's message to them personally?

3. Do they believe that He longs to communicate directly with them through His Word in regard to their personal set of circumstances and place in this world?

These are very important questions that need answering. Again, ask them.

The foundational question "Is God real?" must be answered by us all, and just like all of us, your child must decide if this is true for himself or herself. If they are shaky on this foundational issue, then they are certainly open game for the grenades the world will throw their way.

WHAT THE WORLD IS TELLING YOUR CHILD

Let's take a look at what the world is telling them about God and the Bible. Then, after you look at this worldly view, you must honestly look at your child and see if you can objectively discern which view of God and His Word best describes your child's view.

The world says that while there *may* be only one God, *the chances are slim.* In fact, there are probably many gods. Better yet, we may be gods in the making. If there is only one God, then *there are undoubtedly many ways to reach that God.* In fact, to say there is only one way, such as through Jesus Christ, is not only antiquated, narrow-minded, and intolerant, but it is also a destructive and divisive force in our modern-day society. Some even liken this "extremist" point of view to that of religious radicals such as the Taliban. In fact, in the wake of the September 11 tragic attack on our nation, a major newspaper ran a picture of Pat Robertson and Jerry Falwell, and the caption under the picture said, "The American Taliban."[2]

Your child will be told that *true* education doesn't fill your head with other thoughts but rather should just teach you *how* to think so you can formulate *your own beliefs* about right and wrong, truth and justice, religion and science. Now, you may be thinking, "That doesn't sound so bad." Well, what they don't tell you is that this is the first step to opening your child's mind to make it fertile ground to fill with the doctrine of modern man—a mind absent the presence of eternal perspective, a Christian worldview, or biblical truth, a mind fraught with the deadly dogma of self-actualization, post-modernism, and existentialism.

Dear parent, I cannot convey to you enough the importance of guarding your child's mind. I cannot find enough words to convey to you the importance of filling those young, fertile minds with "whatever is true, whatever is noble, whatever is right, whatever is pure, whatever is lovely, whatever is admirable…excellent or praiseworthy" (Phil. 4:8). Teach them that God and His truth have nothing to fear from investigation and will always and ultimately prevail. Teach them that the truth is only made stronger by the pursuits of a man or woman whose mind is open to the things of Christ. Tell them that belief in God does not discount science, knowledge, and logic but rather a humble belief that it is science and the human mind that must do the catching up to the mind of God.

Peer Factor

Now let's consider the greatest influence on your child: other children. In the midst of all these confusing questions, children are surrounded by their peers whom they care deeply about. Suddenly, and many times without warning, our children are forced to examine the claims of the Bible through their friends' eyes. Such a claim says that the wages of sin is death and that their friends must accept Jesus Christ as their Savior or spend an eternity separated from God in a place called hell. Suddenly, the path to heaven becomes a very narrow passage.

Add to that perspectives from friends, teachers, professors, and the media that proclaim one hundred reasons why the Bible could not possibly be true or applicable for today's society, beginning with the first chapter of Genesis and ending with the fairy-tale "scare tactic" called Revelation, and you have the recipe for *doubt*. Doubt then becomes the door that the world comes through with the specific goal of replacing doubt with the mind of man—reason, feelings, and false teaching.

The Fairness Doctrine

One of the toughest obstacles your child must overcome comes in the form of a simple question that will be posed to them by nearly every non-Christian friend and secular university professor they will ever encounter: How could a loving and merciful God send good people to hell just because they don't share the same beliefs as a Christian? This is followed closely by the next seemingly reasonable question that is asked: Isn't it possible that there are many types of people and cultures and therefore many paths to the same God? Fairness and reasonableness are the foundational issues they will be confronted with day in and day out, all played out in the court of public opinion. What will they say? How will they respond? How will these questions and the pressure that will accompany these questions from their peers affect your child?

Is God Real or Just One Perspective?

This issue of belief comes down to whether your child believes that God, the Father of Jesus Christ, is who we say He is or simply a nice idea. Is He really God, or is He like Santa Claus and the tooth fairy. While they both serve good and noble purposes, are they really just parents' way of convincing us what to believe in to get us to do and be what they want us to do and be? Tough questions indeed but necessary nonetheless. Now, muster up your courage, and go have the conversations. Ask the questions, or at least some of them, and pray for discernment. God will grant it.

chapter 7

CAUSE FOR UNBELIEF (PART 2): NOT YET EXPERIENCED HIS PRESENCE

Physical strength can never permanently withstand the impact of spiritual force.[1]

—FRANKLIN D. ROOSEVELT

A T FIRST GLANCE the question, Has your child experienced the presence of God? seems highly philosophical or abstract. But what I am referring to is very concrete, rubber-meets-the-road kind of stuff. Has your child stood in the presence of his or her personal Lord and Savior, Jesus Christ? Again, the best way I know to help you evaluate this is in the form of two sets of questions that apply to two kinds of experiences. You will have to, again, try to objectively discern which category best describes your child.

LOOKING BENEATH THE SURFACE

Now, I must give a warning. Some of these questions may not be age appropriate for your personal situation, and that is OK. At the very least, you will see the ground you will need to cover in the years ahead as well as the signs to watch for as the years go by. But I should also warn you that most parents assume a maturity and understanding level far below what is actually true.

So you may find yourself surprised to find your child has considered more than you would think.

Questions (circle *yes* or *no*):

Has your child experienced a situation or set of circumstances that truly put his or her beliefs to the test?	yes	no
Has your child ever been in a situation where he or she was totally dependent on God?	yes	no
Has your child been involved in situations where divine intervention is the only explanation for what happened, and were they allowed to later acknowledge the role the Lord played in that situation?	yes	no
Has your child seen the presence, power, and provision of the Lord modeled in your life?	yes	no
If yes, was that acknowledged and discussed until it was fully understood that it was God who sustained you?	yes	no
Has your child stood in the presence of God in the form of either prayer or worship and truly sensed the presence and the power of the Holy Spirit?	yes	no
If yes, was there discussion affirming this and understanding what was happening?	yes	no
Has he or she stood in beautiful places and witnessed the beauty and majesty of God's creation and sensed not only His presence but His imprint as well on all that they surveyed?	yes	no
Has your child witnessed you on your knees before God in prayer seeking God's wisdom and power for their lives?	yes	no
Do they know the trials and struggles that only He got you through?	yes	no

Do they know your testimony?	yes	no
Do they know how Christ has changed you?	yes	no
Can your child honestly say they know the Lord spoke directly to them?	yes	no
Does he or she believe God can do just that?	yes	no

Or, on the other hand:

Is church and religious stuff more of a duty and obligation?	yes	no
Do they have all that they need (material possessions), thereby eliminating dependence on God in their mind?	yes	no
Do they see you attend church on Sundays but live like the rest of the world Monday through Saturday?	yes	no

For older children and teenagers:

Do they do the church stuff with their church friends when it's church time but spend the rest of the time in the world with their non-Christian friends?	yes	no
What do they see when they look at their unsaved friends? Ask them.		
Is hypocrisy and judgmentalism their chief and oft-repeated complaint regarding the church?	yes	no
Is sarcasm and cynicism present in their comments and general outlook on life?	yes	no

Now, let's pause right here for a moment. You may be thinking, "What in the world does judgmentalism and hypocrisy have to do with whether or not my child has stood in the presence of God?" Well, this is the point precisely. *It speaks to whose presence they are standing in.* If they are standing in the presence of sinful man only, then they will see imperfect men and women, hypocrites, sinful man. But if they are truly standing in the presence of their God and Savior, He is none of those sinful things. His love is perfect, His ways are amazing, and His presence intense. All of which invoke an entirely different set of responses, feelings, and attitudes. *Which set of descriptors describes your child?* Pause and reflect on your past observations before answering this next question.

When your child is in church, is he or she (in his or her own mind) standing in the presence of God or merely the presence of imperfect men and women who are called Christians?	yes	no

As I have stated, there is a profound difference. It is the difference between wonder, awe, and joy versus criticism, cynicism, and sarcasm.

Here are more questions to consider:

Have you ever taken the time to watch your child when he or she is listening to a speaker or pastor?	yes	no
When they talk about their future plans, are you in them?	yes	no
When they talk about their future plans, is God in them?	yes	no
Here's a tough one. Do they have more than one master?	yes	no

Here are a few suggestions on how to find out if your child has more than one master.

1. Go to their car and check the buttons for the radio stations they listen to.

2. Look at the lyrics of the CDs in their collection.

3. Watch them sing in church and then watch them sing along in their car and compare the level of intensity or attachment.

Sound freaky? Sound like Big Brother, the CIA, or the fun police? That is not my intention with these questions, nor should it be yours. But what I am ultimately seeking to help you discover is how well you know your kids. Believe me when I tell you that our churches are full of parents who think they did but wish they could have a "do over" so that they could more certainly know that they know their children.

Now, I know you probably think these ideas sound incredibly intrusive and extreme, but what they help you determine is this: in whose presence have your children chosen to stand?

THE THREE MOST IMPORTANT QUESTIONS EVERY PARENT SHOULD CONSIDER

The next three questions may be the most important questions you will answer in this entire book. They relate to each of your children's personalities, strengths, and weaknesses and reflect the reality that there are two forces at work in this world: good and evil. I urge you to make the answers to these questions the focus of every prayer you ever pray for your child. I urge you to not rush through this brief section. These questions should be the very place you stand guard as you strive to protect what God has placed in your hands.

1. Knowing what you know about your child and your family's situation, how do you suppose Satan would go about keeping your child from Christ?

_____

_____

_____

2. How would Satan keep your child from thinking God is real?

_____

_____

_____

3. How would Satan keep your child from standing in the presence of God?

_____

_____

_____

The answers to these questions are incredibly critical to the future of your child. Take the next half hour or so to consider your responses to each question. Then write out your responses and what you have learned in the blanks. If nothing else, write about what has been revealed to you through this process.

chapter 8

THE FAMILY OF GOD

A great and wondrous sign appeared in heaven: a woman clothed with the sun, with the moon under her feet and a crown of twelve stars on her head. She was pregnant and cried out in pain as she was about to give birth. Then another sign appeared in heaven: an enormous red dragon with seven heads and ten horns and seven crowns on his heads...The dragon stood in front of the woman who was about to give birth, so that he might devour her child the moment it was born.

She gave birth to a son, a male child, who will rule all the nations with an iron scepter...And there was war in heaven. Michael and his angels fought against the dragon, and the dragon and his angels fought back. But he was not strong enough, and they lost their place in heaven...

Then the dragon was enraged at the woman and went off to make war against the rest of her offspring—those who obey God's commandments and hold to the testimony of Jesus.

—REVELATION 12:1–5, 7–8, 17

JUST KNOW AND believe this. *The war for the souls of our children* may be manifested in this physical world, but it has its origins in the spirit realm. The battle is at fever pitch, and the enemy's goal is to wrestle your child away from you. Many times, this pursuit takes place in the most subtle ways.

Right now, I believe the Christian family is a slumbering giant. Many prominent Christian leaders are saying the same thing. We are working, playing, and enjoying life as never before, thinking, "All is well. All is well," while we are systematically losing what we hold dearest—our children.

We must wake up, open our eyes, and ask God to reveal His truth to us. We must intercede on behalf of our children and ask that the truth about who they are and whose they are be revealed to us. Then, we must boldly do what God leads us to do.

By now, if you are like many parents, you are probably saying, "My goodness, I am not sure where I stand on most of the questions related to the first two causes. This is too much." And to that I would say, you are right. But hang on because there is good news ahead. There is great hope. There is great victory, and the battle is a just one.

But for now, you must make a decision about all you have read and pondered. Either this book is merely making mountains out of molehills or there really is a problem—a battle that is raging. If you have come to the place where you are the least convinced that there could be a problem, then you are heading in the right direction.

You Are the Difference Maker

The place to begin is with you, the parent, because you truly are the difference. In fact, Scripture charges you with doing just that: making a difference in the life of God's precious gift to you—His children.

> By wisdom a house is built, and through understanding it is established; through knowledge its rooms are filled with rare and beautiful treasures.
>
> —PROVERBS 24:3–4

> Only be careful, and watch yourselves closely so that you do not forget the things your eyes have seen or let them slip from your

heart as long as you live. Teach them to your children and to their children after them.

—DEUTERONOMY 4:9

There are some bridges you must cross and perhaps a few you may need to burn as you gird yourself for the battle that you are already in. More about your walk as a parent and a believer will be discussed in a later chapter.

POWERFUL PAUSE AND REFLECTION

The final focus of this section examines the third major cause for unbelief in our families: the world and all it's alluring appeal. But before you dive into the next chapter, I would like to make an appeal to you to stop for a moment, put the book down, get before your God in humble adoration and powerful praise for all He is and all He has done, and then just pour out your heart before Him concerning your children. God inhabits the praise of His people, and He hears every heartfelt prayer of His children, especially those that come from parents. Pray for wisdom. Pray for discernment. *Pray for revelation.* Then pray for strength, for His power, and for victory. This is next-level stuff. Powerful stuff!

After you pray, be sure to allow your mind and heart time to process and reflect on what God is saying to you at this point in the journey. Take a moment to reflect and write down what God has shown you or spoken to you about. Maybe spend some time with your spouse in discussion and discovery. But allow for God to come in and reveal His thoughts, insights, and will to you at this critical point in your journey.

chapter 9

CAUSE FOR UNBELIEF (PART 3): THE WORLD IS AN ATTRACTIVE PLACE

The young, with their keen noses for hypocrisy, are in fact adept readers—but not of books. They are society-smart rather than school-smart, and what they read so acutely are the social signals emanating from the world in which they will have to make a living. Their teachers in that world, the nation's true pedagogues, are television, advertising, movies, politics, and the celebrity domains they define. We prattle about deficient schools and the gullible youngsters they turn out, so vulnerable to the siren song of drugs, but think nothing of letting the advertisers into the classroom to fashion what an Advertising Age essay calls "brand and product loyalties through classroom-centered, peer-powered lifestyle patterning."[1]

—BENJAMIN BARBER
WALT WHITMAN PROFESSOR OF POLITICAL SCIENCE,
DIRECTOR OF THE WHITMAN CENTER
AT RUTGERS UNIVERSITY

THE WORLD HAS become so incredibly and remarkably attractive to our physical mind that it has captured our attention, but the real danger lies in the fact that for many of us, and our children, it has captured our affections.

In a newsletter from Focus on the Family, Kurt Bruner, vice president in charge of the Focus Resource Group at Focus on the Family, stated the following:

> Our children are growing up in a popular culture that often goes out of its way to attack and belittle the Christian faith. Clearly, the culture is becoming more and more hostile to our faith, which makes our task as parents increasingly difficult. A recent survey of Focus on the Family listeners revealed that finding help for the spiritual development of their children was their number-one need.[2]

In the same month this article was published, Focus on the Family launched a cutting-edge new ministry called Heritage Builders. The ministry was designed to educate, train, and equip parents to become intentional about passing on a spiritual heritage to their children.

Through marketing, demographics, and target programming, the media has made the world appear like an incredibly attractive place. But whether or not you believe the problem is as pervasive as I do, what matters most is what is true for your child. You must seek to know the truth about where your child is spiritually, emotionally, and in their understanding of what matters most in life. Where are their affections? What is their mind set upon? What do they love? What do they fear? How can you know?

> We live in a culture where our young people hear with their eyes and think with their heart.[3]
>
> —Ravi Zacharias

I have designed a set of questions I would encourage you to work through with your child. The list of questions is designed to help you see inside their heart and mind. You do not have to work through all of these questions in one sitting. You may want to pick and choose which questions you would like to focus on. But the goal is simple: to encourage courageous, open, and honest conversations. Don't be surprised at how much your child may be willing to reveal. Most parents are shocked, usually pleasantly, at the candid responses they receive when they just ask the right questions. It seems our children have experienced more of life than we thought and have formed some very definite thoughts and opinions about their plans for the future. It turns out that they are not the quiet observers we thought them to be, but rather they are very much aware and acutely tuned in to the comings and goings of their world.

Another caution I want to give you before you start is to *not* make each question a time to provide a lengthy lecture. It is also not the time to give a dissertation of your responses to each question (unless they ask, which rarely occurs during this process). Remember, the goal is discovery, truth, and revelation about *who* your child is as well as *whose* your child is.

I have found that the best time to ask my own girls these questions is when we are having our prayer time, when I tuck them in their beds, or while we are driving somewhere together in the car. All four of my girls are different, and I have learned to adjust my approach for each personality.

Whatever approach you choose, it is important that you find a starting place and go. Run the race. Ask the tough questions. Listen with your eyes and ears. Take good notes, and maybe even consider taping the responses. Take to heart what you hear. You may find that you will get better responses if you let your children know the questions you are going to ask ahead of time. This allows them to have time to process their thoughts before actually having to answer the questions.

LOOKING BENEATH THE SURFACE

1. If someone gave you forty million dollars, what would you do with it? (I have learned not to ask what they will buy because for some, saving it for something later is very important, which is a very telling response as well.)

2. What kind of things do you love?

3. What kind of things do you hate?

4. What kind of things do you fear?

5. What kind of things do you need?

6. If you could change three things about yourself, what would you change?

7. What are your favorite two or three songs? Why?

8. What are your favorite two or three television shows? Why?

9. What characters in your favorite shows do you identify with the most? Why?

10. Whom do you respect most (two or three people), and why?

11. If you could ask God three questions, what would you ask? Why?

12. Do you think you have enemies? Who, and why?

13. What does God see when He looks at you? Explain.

14. What do you see when you think about God?

15. What things do you treasure most?

16. What are the best three things about you?

17. What are the worst two things about you?

18. What would you attempt if you knew you could not fail?

19. If you could change three things about your church, what would you change?

20. If you could go anywhere in the world for two weeks, where would you go? Why?

21. What moves you most? (Be prepared to define *moves*.)

Now, I know that most of you are really squirming in your seats right now just pondering such conversations with your child. But can you see the depths you will be able to plumb if you can discuss even just a few of these questions? Remember, you don't have to ask them all in one sitting, as this does not have to be an interview. It is, rather, more of an *inner view* and one that must be worked through after prayer and with an open mind to what you might learn. I would suggest focusing on a set of five to eight questions at a time, with the emphasis being more on discussion and less on just answers to the questions. Ask your questions, and then, rather than give thoughts or opinions, just ask more follow-up questions with a goal of clarity and understanding. Lastly, please keep in mind, you must not be in pursuit of self-approval. *This isn't about you ... yet.*

After listening and reflecting, you must seek to understand whom they serve—God or man. This is so incredibly important to this process as the answer to this question must serve as the basis for every point of action you undertake from here forward. As you reflect on their answers, ask yourself:

- Where is my child's focus? Is it on God or man?

- Who is his or her audience? Is it God or man?

- Who does he or she spend time with? Is it God or man?

- Who has his or her day? Is it God or man?

- Who and what does he or she value? Is it God, or is it man?

- Where does his or her wildest dreams take him or her? Closer to God or deeper into the world?

And, lastly the most important question of all:

- Who does he or she fear, revere? Who does he or she hold in highest regard? Is it God or man?

Hopefully, your child has given you enough information for you to know whether God or man is lording over them. Now you have an important choice to make.

chapter 10

THE FORK IN THE ROAD

Human progress is neither automatic nor inevitable...Every step toward the goal of justice requires sacrifice, suffering, and struggle; the tireless exertions and passionate concern of dedicated individuals.[1]

—MARTIN LUTHER KING JR.

ASED ON WHAT you have discovered up to this point about your child, you have a choice to make today. Who will raise your child? Who will be their lord? Will it be your God, your Lord and Savior, or will it be the deceiver, the one who has captured the imaginations of so many and placed his set of values in the hearts of men that he might lead them astray?

You must step up in a mighty and bold way. If you have decided that your child will be raised up knowing that God is Lord of their lives, you have just declared war on the enemy, and now you must commit to parent at the next level...in the spirit realm, where that war is raging *right now* for the souls of your children.

Over the last ten years I have had the privilege of serving as a professor on a few university campuses across the nation. The first several years, I taught as an adjunct professor two evenings per week while I worked as a high school administrator by day. It had been a dream of mine for many years to be a full-time university professor. When I finally got the opportunity to do this, I jumped at the chance. It required that I tote my family off to a small rural college town in the Midwest, into what we called "our great adventure." It was no easy thing to leave sunny Southern California, the only place our three children had ever known as home, but we went for it.

As my family and I made the switch from city life to rural life, I also made the switch from K-12 education life to university climate, culture, and student life. The town where we lived was predominately a different religion than our own, but we did manage to find a small Baptist church. It was one of only a handful of evangelical churches within a fifty-mile radius. That was a radical change in and of itself as we had just left our home church of the past eight years that had a weekly attendance of over seven thousand, and out of that large church came every ministry imaginable. But God provided in extraordinary ways, and we found our small-town life to be a refreshing, safe, and very comforting existence. We also saw God move in incredible ways during our two years there.

My life as a full-time university professor was an altogether different experience. I loved my time with the students. I was able to teach and serve in extracurricular activities in addition to facilitating a campus Bible study that my wife and I led once a week. But what I wasn't ready for was the level of intensity with which evangelical values and beliefs were being assaulted in some of the classrooms, or the opposition to the Christian faith I encountered in monthly faculty meetings.

The Lord led me to a few other born-again professors who had been hunkering down in their bunkers just trying to survive the storm for years. I found out in just my first semester there that this university campus was one of the fiercest battlegrounds where the war was raging for the souls of young men and women.

Over the course of the second semester, through much research, reading, and observation, I discovered that it wasn't just the university campus where I was serving, but it was also nearly every secular university campus in America. The Lord opened my eyes and showed me in great detail how this war on college and university campuses is not only for the souls of the students but ultimately for the heart of this great nation. You see, what the Lord showed me was what many of my Christian contemporaries had been saying for several years: *as the universities of this country go, so goes the spiritual health of this nation.* God is watching.

Students are seldom challenged with the simple question, What is the truth? For many students in our institutions of higher learning, what is being taught is that what matters most is not what is ultimately true but rather what they have discovered to be true "for themselves." Thus, all truth is relative, and all truth is subjective. Therefore, what is true for one may not be true for another. Nothing transcends, and nothing is absolute. Yet, here is the greatest tragedy: truth, as it is being taught in far too many places of learning, can only be found in what one discovers with his or her limited time, resources, and experiences.

What should be taught is the objective pursuit of timeless, transcending truth, regardless of what one's subjective and limited view of reality might be at any fixed point in time. Science, however advanced it may appear to be in any given year, is infinitely more advanced than what it was fifty years ago. And, conversely, what science is today is infinitely less than it will be in fifty more years. We must make an allowance for the possibility that it is science and the mind of man that need to catch up to the God of the universe and not the other way around. What should be the hallmark of every institution of higher learning is the pursuit of truth and a core belief that says *the truth about anything has nothing to fear from investigation.*

But this is a truth that requires a surrendering of one's own agenda and yields to a higher, divine law where there is true fairness, true justice, and true love. What this kind of truth requires is simply not an option in far too many halls of academia, and that is faith. Faith is the antithesis of existentialism. They simply cannot coexist.

Existentialism is defined as "A philosophical attitude that stresses the individual's unique position as a self-determining agent, responsible for the authenticity of his or her own choices and experiences absent the existence of a higher authority."

Far too many have sadly exchanged the truth for a lie. I believe those responsible for this indoctrination and exploitation will be held responsible by a God who sees and hears all. To think your child would not be confronted with this same assault is naïve…at best. That is the same God who created this young man with a very specific purpose and plan that includes a relationship with Him and a life of hope and great promise. This new life will be based on real truth that passes all the tests—historical, scientific, *and* spiritual.

TWO WORLDVIEWS COLLIDE

The world, over the last fifty years or so, has taken the very core beliefs of Christianity and rejected each emphatically—the Virgin Birth, the Crucifixion, the Resurrection, Christ's sinless life and sacrifice, Jesus as God, the miracles…and that's just the beginning. The world uses so-called knowledge and intellect to refute Christian beliefs, but what I am about to show you from a biblical standpoint says something very different from what the world says concerning the kind of knowledge we need and where it comes from.

In Proverbs 1:7, Scripture says, "The fear of the LORD is the beginning of knowledge." It is clear here that if we want any knowledge at all, it must start with fearing God, but to what knowledge does the scripture refer? What should be our purpose, our goal in gaining knowledge? Again, Scripture is clear:

> [*For my determined purpose is*] that I may know Him [that I may progressively become more deeply and intimately acquainted with Him, perceiving and recognizing and understanding the wonders of His Person more strongly and more clearly], and that I may in that same way come to know the power outflowing from His

resurrection [which it exerts over believers], and that I may so share His sufferings as *to be continually transformed [in spirit into His likeness* even] to His death.

—PHILIPPIANS 3:10, AMP, EMPHASIS ADDED

The keyword in this Scripture verse is *transformed*. This is what we are about as parents. It is in this transformation process that we find victory or defeat. Romans says:

And do not be conformed to this world, but be *transformed* by the renewing of your mind, that you may prove what is that good and acceptable and perfect will of God.

—ROMANS 12:2, NKJV, EMPHASIS ADDED

There's that word again—*transformed*. Rick Warren, in his book *The Purpose-Driven Life*, points out an incredibly important fact about the word *transformed*.

The Greek word for transformed is metamorphosis (used in Romans 12:2 and 2 Corinthians 3:18), *which is used today to describe the amazing change a caterpillar goes through in becoming a butterfly.* It is a beautiful picture of what happens to us spiritually when we allow God to direct our thoughts: We are changed from the inside out, we become more beautiful, and we are set free to soar to new heights.[2]

—EMPHASIS ADDED

Stay with me; we are coming to a very critical point. As I referred to earlier, there is this incredible pull of the world that has held incredible sway over Christians throughout history, and it is again played out in Hosea 4:6: "My people are destroyed from lack of knowledge. Because you have rejected knowledge...because you have ignored the law of your God."

Incredibly, this passage refers to a generation that was destroyed, not because they did not have the knowledge at their fingertips, but because they had it, they looked at it, they pondered it, and then they flatly rejected it. You must understand that we are not talking about any old kind of knowledge. There is a knowledge of good *and* evil. Then there is a knowledge that leads to eternal life. This choice between the world's knowledge and the knowledge that produces life reflects back to the choice Adam and Eve had in the Garden of Eden between eating from the tree of the knowledge of good and evil or eating from the tree of life. The world may have its version of knowledge—that which is formed by the mind of man and his experiences, resources, and limited time—but it only leads to death. The knowledge that begins with fearing God as stated in Proverbs 1:7 and transformation (Phil. 3:10; Rom. 12:2) is what leads to life.

"So what does the message in Hosea and the fall of Adam and Eve have to do with today?" you might ask. Specifically, the verse in Hosea speaks with incredible accuracy about the United States of America. We were once a nation that was not only founded on foundational Christian truth presented in Scripture but also established, as acknowledged by our forefathers, by God's grace and blessing. And by the way, if you have any doubts about this at all, just read the first paragraph of the Declaration of Independence. For more information about these roots and foundational issues and documents, go to the Wall Builders Web site at www .wallbuilders.com. David Barton, the founder of Wall Builders, has made it his life's pursuit and passion to prove this in great detail and with overwhelming evidence.[3] But man has rejected this truth through examination and running it through the courts of our justice system and the courts of popular opinion.

Just to show you that I am not overstating the case, I have put together a list of these beliefs that started our nation on its course to greatness but have since been rejected. These are fundamentals that were once part of our everyday lives but have been taken from the public eye within my lifetime and yours.

THE VERDICT

Prayer in schools	Rejected
Ten Commandments displayed	Rejected
Presence of a Creator in science	Rejected
Creationism as a truth	Rejected
Creationism as a theory	Rejected
The Virgin Birth	Impossible
A resurrection from the dead	Improbable
Christmas	Rejected
Easter	Rejected
Christian prayer at graduation	Rejected
Christ mentioned in graduation speeches	Rejected
Sanctity of life	Rejected
Right and wrong	Relative
Parents' right to know if their child is going to have an abortion	Rejected
Abstinence	Rejected
Influence of Christian Scripture, principles, and men in the founding documents of this country	Retracted

The list could go on and on. Do you understand what it is I am trying to convey? There will be, for all children, this period of metamorphosis where transformation will take place. We cannot hold those hands of time back. What will fill that period of time for your child? What knowledge will be laid as seed? What will take root?

THE GOAL OF NEXT-LEVEL PARENTS

Our goal is that over time, through the daily interactions with our children and through the interactions with peers and families who share our core beliefs, our children will be transformed into the likeness of Christ and learn to see the world through His eyes, hear with His ears, feel with His heart, and act in His strength. This is why we exist! This should be our determined purpose! This is the goal! Are you up for it?

THE CHALLENGE

Are you willing to stand up for your child even if it means laying down your life? Are you willing to lose some sleep to late-night or early-morning prayer? Are you willing to come home from work when you can, and not just when you want? Are you willing to fall on your knees in humbleness and boldly go before the throne of God and seek His face, His mercy, and His salvation? If you can answer yes to these questions, and if you can even contemplate such an adventure, then there is hope.

British critic A. A. Gill once said this:

> Christianity started out with 11 members and was at its strongest and purest. If it goes back to being 11, or if I'm the only poor creature in the world still afflicted with it, it will make no difference. God will still be there and will love us unrequited. The world was still round when nobody believed it.[4]

You are not alone. You are never alone, and there is victory in this battle, and it is there for the taking. I've seen it with my own eyes in hundreds of families. God does have a plan for you, and He is not surprised by any of this. But you must understand, to do nothing more than go through the motions, in this day and age, could well prove catastrophic. You must—we must—take up arms, spiritual arms, and stand in the gap for our children. God promises to meet us there and to sustain us and to give us victory.

SECTION III

SPIRITUAL SIGNIFICANCE AND HISTORICAL CONTEXT

Those who do not remember the past are condemned to repeat it.[1]

GEORGE SANTAYANA

chapter 11

Signs of the Times

He who controls the past commands the future. He who commands the future conquers the past.[1]

—George Orwell

THE FIRST STEP toward any victory is understanding what you are up against and the historical context of the situation. Therefore, I am going to paint a picture for you in this chapter from a historical perspective of where we are currently as a society. Let's see if you agree.

Now, more than any other time in history, there are greater levels of corruption and violence. Most people no longer seek the counsel of God. They have forgotten the many ways God has intervened for this great country in perilous times. Our generation is stubborn and rebellious. We have become a nation that refuses to walk according to the Law of the Lord.

The people of this day eat, drink, and make merry with more excess than at any other time in modern history. Lust is being played out on Earth at greater levels than at any other point in history, and the pornography industry is increasing in influence day by day. Idolatry is present in many of the modern religions, as well as in a few of the not-so-modern religions. Materialism is at fever pitch as man has created for himself gods of gold and gods of status.

Do any of these descriptions sound vaguely familiar? They should. They are the descriptions of the people who lived right before God brought the

Flood in Noah's time (Gen. 6) and of the people Moses happened upon when he returned from Mt. Sinai with the Ten Commandments (Exod. 32).

The references above are descriptions of the hearts of the people just before God brought judgment upon those people and places. There are great similarities between the times we are in here in the United States and those times when the wrath of God was brought to bear on a stubborn and stiff-necked people. We are a people who are living at the edge of God's patience and at the door of His judgment and wrath. I am not alone in this conclusion, as many of our nations greatest Christian leaders would agree and have proclaimed the very same thing from their pulpits and television and radio programs.

> This know also, that in the last days perilous times shall come. For men shall be lovers of their own selves, covetous, boasters, proud, blasphemers, disobedient to parents, unthankful, unholy, without natural affection, trucebreakers, false accusers, incontinent, fierce, despisers of those that are good, traitors, heady, highminded, lovers of pleasures more than lovers of God.
>
> —2 TIMOTHY 3:1–4, KJV

And here is the clincher for the church:

> *Having a form of godliness, but denying the power thereof*…laden with sins, led away with divers lusts, ever learning, and never able to come to the knowledge of the truth…deceiving, and being deceived.
>
> —2 TIMOTHY 3:5–7, 13, KJV, EMPHASIS ADDED

We as a nation are treading on very thin moral and spiritual ice. But we must praise God, for He has told us in His Word, "If my people, which are called by my name, shall humble themselves, and pray, and seek my face…then will I hear from heaven, and will forgive their sin, and will heal their land" (2 Chron. 7:14, KJV).

How About Our Generation?

The first big question that begs to be asked has to be, How did we get to where we are today? How did we allow ourselves, one of the greatest, if not *the* greatest, nations, a nation founded on Christian principles, stray so far from the center of God's will? Once again, I think the answer lies in the Word of God. There is an absolutely beautiful passage of Scripture in Deuteronomy 6 that has one of the best prescriptions for success I have found in the Bible. I will begin with the second half of the passage to show the effects, prior to showing the remedy.

> So it shall be, when the LORD your God brings you into the land of which He swore to your fathers, to Abraham, Isaac, and Jacob, to give *you large and beautiful cities which you did not build, houses full of all good things, which you did not fill, hewn-out wells which you did not dig, vineyards and olive trees which you did not plant*—when you have eaten and are full—then beware, lest you forget the LORD who brought you out of the land of Egypt, from the house of bondage. You shall fear the LORD your God and serve Him, and shall take oaths in His name. You shall not go after other gods, the gods of the peoples who are all around you (for the LORD your God is a jealous God among you), lest the anger of the LORD your God be aroused against you and destroy you from the face of the earth. You shall not tempt the LORD your God as you tempted Him in Massah.
>
> —DEUTERONOMY 6:10–16, NKJV, EMPHASIS ADDED

Parents in the 2000s, for the most part, are the first generation removed from the fear of losing our way of life to a foreign power. September 11 certainly caused an awakening, for a time. But, according to studies done on this topic, only a year or so after one of the greatest tragedies of our modern times, life went on pretty much the same as it did before that fateful day.

We have not endured a depression or world wars anywhere near the gravity of what this country endured in generations past. We are the generation that had parents who worked so very diligently to give us all of the things that they did not have so that we would not know the hardship they knew growing up.

We are parents of children who inhabit large and beautiful cities they did not build, live in houses full of good things they did not help to fill, and drink and eat of all good things they did not have to help provide. They don't wake up to any real threat of losing their freedom. In fact, the sheltered existence we have been blessed to provide our children with has resulted in a generation whose focus has shifted from survival and pioneering to enjoyment and the pursuit of happiness.

Tragically, we have succeeded in eliminating the need for God in the minds of our children. They have all they need and most of what they want. And as long as our children see their existence with physical eyes only, this whole "need" thing is illogical or intolerant.

THE ABUNDANCE FACTOR

For many of you, the battle might not be found in your family's struggles or hard times at all. For many families, the best way to keep you from depending on God is by giving you financial freedom or comfort enough that your child never has to rely on God's provision. Scripture says, "It is easier for a camel to go through the eye of a needle than for a rich man to enter the kingdom of God" (Matt. 19:24; cf. Mark 10:25; Luke 18:25). Why? Because, quite simply, it is hard to find on their knees men or women who think they have need of nothing. And I would add that for your children, this is substantially magnified.

Have you ever considered that Satan could see to it that you rarely have tragedy or poor health or financial strains at all? That way you would not need to rely on God's strength, comfort, or provision. *Could this be you?* Could the very thing you think you have been so abundantly blessed with be the very reason you or your child has yet to stand in God's presence? I can tell you story after story of wealthy Christian men and women who have lost their children to the world. They would give all their wealth away in a heart-beat to have another chance at doing it differently.

Newsweek magazine recently published an article called, "The Challenge: Just Say No," and in this article some of their research findings were startling.[2]

> It's an unexpected legacy of the affluent 90's: parents who can't say no…This generation of parents has always been driven to give their kids every advantage, from Mommy and Me swim classes all the way to that thick envelope from an elite college. But despite their good intentions, too many find themselves raising "wanting machines" who respond like Pavlovian dogs to the marketing behemoth that's aimed right at them. Now a growing number of psychologists, educators, and parents think it's time to stop the madness and start teaching kids about what's really important—values like hard work, delayed gratification, honesty, and compassion…Kids who've been given too much too soon grow up to be adults who have a difficulty coping with life's disappointments. They have a distorted sense of entitlement that gets in the way of success both in the workplace and in relationships.

A few facts to consider:

- Families with three- to twelve-year-olds spend $53.8 billion annually on entertainment, personal-care items, and reading materials, which is $17.6 billion more than parents spent in 1997.

- Twelve- to nineteen-year-olds spent roughly $175 billion, which is $53 billion more than in 1997.[3]

William Damon, director of the Stanford University Center on Adolescence, says, "The risk of over-indulgence is self-centeredness and self-absorption, and that's a mental-health risk. You sit around feeling anxious all the time instead of figuring out what you can do to make a difference in the world."[4]

Money does not have to be the key factor here. You do not have to be wealthy to be overly permissive. You do not have to use money to overindulge a child.

According to the article mentioned above, "today's parents put in more hours on the job too; at the end of a long workweek, it's tempting to buy peace with a 'yes,' rather than mar precious family time with conflict. One survey of grade-school children found that when they crave something new, most expect to ask nine times before their parents give in. Experts agree: too much love won't spoil a child, but too few limits will."[5]

What about you? What about your family? Before you answer, the Book of Judges holds another powerful statement:

> And also all that generation were gathered unto their fathers: and there arose another generation after them, which knew not the LORD, nor yet the works which he had done for Israel. And the children of Israel did evil in the sight of the LORD, and served Baalim: and they forsook the LORD God of their fathers, which brought them out of the land of Egypt, and followed other gods, the gods of the people that were round about them, and bowed themselves unto them, and provoked the LORD to anger. And they forsook the LORD, and served Baal and Ashtaroth.
>
> —JUDGES 2:10–13, KJV

THE LAW OF GENERATIONAL DECLINE

How incredibly tragic to see a generation so close in behavior to the very generation of people God personally delivered out of Egyptian slavery. How could this be? You need to know that there is instance after instance where this occurs in the Bible, and the most critical time where this consistently occurs is in the passing of one generation to another. This phenomenon is referred to as "the law of generational decline." While I do not claim to have invented this title or law, I use it practically to describe an occurrence that happens again and again in the Bible, beginning with Adam and continuing today in the life of the modern Christian church. Jim Cymbala, in his book *Fresh Wind, Fresh Fire* (a must-read for every Christian parent and pastor on the planet), describes it the following way:

> Solomon, as everyone knows, had wandered from God near the end of His life. Rehoboam, who came next, and then Abijah, Asa's father, let idol worship come right into the midst of what was supposed to be a godly society. Baal was welcomed as a help to the crops; Asherah poles, oversized carvings of the male sex organ supposed to bring fertility, were common; children were actually offered as sacrifices in the fires of Molech.[6]

Now, please be careful to note that Abijah was only three generations removed from the person God called "a man after my own heart" (Acts 13:22). That's right, Solomon was David's son and Abijah's grandfather. Just the drifting away from the foundational truths Solomon had been taught and knew caused the first step of decline. This decline would result in utter idol worship and blasphemy before God just a few generations later.

The story continues in I Kings 11:4–6: "As Solomon grew old, his wives turned his heart after other gods, and his heart was not fully devoted to the LORD his God, as the heart of David his father had been. He followed Ashtoreth the goddess of the Sidonians, and Molech the detestable god of the Ammonites. So Solomon did evil in the eyes of the LORD; he did not follow the LORD completely, as David his father had done." This is amazing! This is Solomon, the son of David. This is the same Solomon who, earlier in his life, had spoken directly with God. But as relationships with seemingly good people with the most harmless of intentions begin to deepen, Solomon's separation increased. It increased to place where this king eventually bowed down before the false gods of Ashtoreth and Molech.

WHAT DOES THIS HAVE TO DO WITH *MY* CHILD?

You may be asking yourself this question. I think that the connections are incredible, and the message of the Bible speaks again and again throughout all generations. Now, I wonder what the kings we have talked about—Solomon, Rehoboam, and Abijah—were like as children. I wonder if they were obedient and respectful to their parents. I wonder if they did all of their chores and did well in their studies. I wonder if they came home when they were supposed to and they told their mother and father that they loved them. I wonder if they kept the laws of the land and if they were respectful toward authority. How different were these children from our definition of "a great kid"?

The task we must undertake as parents is twofold. First, we must have the courage and seek to really know the truth about who our children are. Second, we must heed the admonishment from Scripture that tells us we must take on the role of educator in our homes.

Can you see why so many of our nation's religious leaders, biblical scholars, and pastors are so concerned? Can you see why they are increasingly devoting so much of their time and prayer life to asking God to stay His hand of judgment on this nation? They can see it. They have seen the symptoms of apathy in their congregations and in their church families. They have seen it in their church's youth ministries. They have sensed it trying to creep into their times of worship. Those who are praying know where the war is. Those who discern the movement of Satan know where to focus their prayers and energies. In his book *Boiling Point*, George Barna, Christian researcher and student of American trends, discusses how "America is rapidly devolving into a society beset by moral anarchy...[and] moral anarchy has arrived and rules our culture today. The argument hinges on a substantial amount of attitudinal and behavioral evidence: record bankruptcy levels, frivolous lawsuits, the rapid growth of the pornography industry, highway speeding as the norm, income tax cheating, computer hacking and viruses, rising levels of white collar crime, rampant copyright violations (movies, books, recordings), terrorism and intimidation tactics, Net-based plagiarism, emotional comfort with lying and cheating, increasing rates of co-habitation and adultery, and so forth."[7]

THE CHURCH—GOD'S INSTRUMENT OF HOPE FOR THE WORLD

The evidence is overwhelming. Were it not for Christians in this country and around the world on their knees daily seeking God's mercy, there would be little that would stand between sinful man and a righteous and just God. But I want to also proclaim that I have personally stood in congregations across this country where they are winning this war. Their youth programs are alive and vibrant. Their worship is filled with excitement, enthusiasm, and joy. Scripture is being proclaimed with boldness and power, and the lost are being found and redeemed. God is alive and moving in their midst, and they are experiencing victory. There is hope, there is joy, and there is redemptive community! I have seen it.

But I have been in the other congregations as well. It is no small thing that there are as many churches in this country closing their doors as there are new ones that are starting. Once healthy and vibrant cathedrals, worship centers now sit empty or are sold to some private business venture.

I have seen both sides of this coin in the Christian families of this country as well. I have personally met and known families who are experiencing victory, and their testimonies are incredible. They have run the race and finished the course laid before them. Yes, there was sacrifice, and no, it was not an easy victory. But they all say two things time and again: (1) it was worth every sacrifice, every fast, every sleepover, every late-night talk when they were tired, every moment in prayer. It was worth it. (2) Time flies. I have heard many say things like, "It was here and then gone in a flash, in a whisper." Most sentences begin with, "Why, it seems like just yesterday that..."

But please believe me when I say that I have seen the other side of the coin where there is devastation, broken lives, deep wounds, and tragic consequences. And they tend to say the same things as well. The most notable being, "If I could only have another chance, I would have done…" That is followed all too often by "Where did it all go wrong?"

Which description will describe you when it is all said and done? Will you stay where you are, or will you reach for a star? Will you simply go through the motions, or will you dare to parent at the next level? The choice is yours, so choose wisely while there is still time.

chapter 12

THE GENERATIONAL DIVIDE: BEYOND THE IRON CURTAIN

It is my personal approach that creates the climate. It is my
daily mood that makes the weather...I possess tremendous
power to make a child's life miserable or joyous. I can be a tool
of torture or an instrument of inspiration. I can humiliate or
humor, hurt or heal. In all situations, it is my response that
decides whether a crisis will be escalated or de-escalated and
a child humanized or de-humanized.[1]

—HAIM GINOTT

Nothing is ever achieved without enthusiasm.[2]

—RALPH WALDO EMERSON

I**T IS ALWAYS** amazing to me when I hear parents talk about their
ability, or lack thereof, to relate to their children. While there are
those who are the exception, most parents, in general, feel that they
are quite a bit removed from their child's generation. When I conduct
the Next Level conferences, one of my favorite activities is what I call
"Memory Lane." I use this activity to illustrate to my audience that the
generational divide may not be as broad an expanse as they might think.

As you work through this exercise, take your time, and take in the full
memory of the moment. Allow yourself to read each item slowly, and then
pause and reflect for as long as you need to for each item that stirs a memory.

Think of the sights, smells, feelings, routines, and all the "stuff" that was your life. This is so much easier to do in the conference because I have each person close their eyes and then I walk them through the exercise. But I am going to trust that you will not rush through and that you will embrace the moment as one that is important and significant. The focus is high school, so set your memory bank for that time in your life.

MEMORY LANE

Below is a list of memories. Read each one. Pause, reflect, and remember.

Pimples	The fair
Favorite teachers	First driving lesson
Love letters	First car
Lockers	First ticket
"Mommy" becoming "Mom"	School dances
Clothing styles	First kiss
Detention	Broken heart
"Daddy" becoming "Dad"	SATs
School food	Curfew
Where you sat at lunch	Crushes
First boyfriend or girlfriend	Being alone
Training bra	The driving test
Best friends	Church
Favorite radio station	God
Jock strap	Jesus
Bullies	Youth group
Favorite songs	Parties

The phone	Homecoming
Freshman year	Prom
Toilet papering a house	Choosing a college
Senior year	Pictures in your wallet/purse
Hairstyles	Yearbooks
Lip gloss	Waiting for the phone to ring
Brothers	Curfew
Pep rallies	Graduation
Sports	PE
Sisters	Long phone conversations
The movies	Music too loud
Worst teacher	Grounded

How did you do? Any memories or flashbacks? I am here to tell you that every time I do this with a group of people, there are many common experiences. First, I am always told that they are amazed how quickly and vividly they remembered so many of those events. They also tell me that many of the *feelings* they felt back then came flooding up as well.

Then, every group also draws some of the same conclusions about the experience as the previous groups. The first being that they believe the reason for the strong remembrances is because at that time in their lives, those things were *so* important. They also notice in the conferences that when I sprinkle in a few things like math, biology, English, or history class, no memories, no recollection, nothing is there, and they understand the significance of that. They connect the dots with their own kids knowing that what is most important to us isn't so important to them, and it's not nearly as important to them as the stuff that was so important to us when we were their age.

But most importantly, the big revelation is in knowing that nearly all of the items I had you walk down memory lane to remember are all things your kids will go through when it is their turn—the same feelings, events, and, for the most part, the same anxieties, fears, hopes, and dreams as you had. They will also experience the same pains, hurts, failures, setbacks, and broken hearts you had. Both you and your child can connect on the fact that you both will have had the same needs, questions, search for significance, and need for a Savior.

Through this exercise you can see that the bridge between the generations is much shorter and traversable than society would lead you to believe.

Most parents greatly underestimate their ability to influence their children, especially during the tumultuous teenage years. But the facts and the statistics simply do not bear this out. In fact, what study after study shows is that you are the single greatest influence, good or bad, in the life of your child.

The loss of a parent is still the number one fear of a child, and this does not just mean the death of a parent. Teens still say the number one reason they do not try drugs or alcohol is fear of disappointing their parents. As the commercial says, you are the most powerful antidrug on the planet.

You should also know that suicide is still a leading killer of teens in this country, and broken romantic relationships with peers is one of the leading reasons given. This would not be nearly as significant to you as a parent were it not for the fact that many times, the deepest teen romances, with the most tragic of consequences, are the result of attention, love, or affection they were not able to receive from the place God intended it to come from—the home, and more specifically, you.

In the next chapter, there is another activity I want to walk you through that I think you will find extremely revealing. This activity will only take you about five minutes to complete, but it is so critical to your understanding of the real generational divide that exists—or doesn't exist.

chapter 13

RELATIONSHIPS MATTER MOST

If civilization is to survive, we must cultivate the science of human relationships—the ability of all peoples, of all kinds, to live together, in the same world at peace.[1]

—FRANKLIN D. ROOSEVELT

RELATIONSHIP, AS YOU will find throughout this book, is the key to *everything*. Ultimately, everything you learn in this process will be absolutely useless if you are not able to take what you are learning and apply it in your relationships. But I believe with everything in me, no matter how shy or macho you may be, it can be done. Necessity is the mother of invention. I can think of little that is more necessary than for you to deepen your relationship with those you love the most.

Take a moment and walk through the activity on the next few pages. The goal is honest evaluation. It is only through honest evaluation that you can really begin to understand what is missing and what you need to work on. The exercise is called "Rate Your Relationships." Simply rate your relationship with each of your children on a scale from one to ten. Ten would be the perfect relationship. Zero would be as bad as bad gets, or virtually no relationship at all. Then, after rating the relationship(s), I want you to take a moment to list or explain what it would take to move the relationship closer to a ten.

Lastly, I am asking you to do the same thing and rate your relationship with your child's other parent. For some of you, this will be your spouse, but I also realize that for some, this could be a parent that is no longer your spouse because of death, divorce, or separation. Even in the case of the latter, it is imperative that you walk through this exercise. I have found time and again that your relationship with your child's other parent is one of the most critical factors in parenting. Now, take a deep breath, and begin.

Rate your relationship with your oldest child on a scale from one to ten (ten meaning there is no room for improvement). Circle one:

I   2   3   4   5   6   7   8   9   10

Explain what it would take to move this relationship closer to a ten.

_____

_____

_____

_____

Rate your relationship with your second child on a scale from one to ten (ten meaning there is no room for improvement). Circle one:

I   2   3   4   5   6   7   8   9   10

Explain what it would take to move this relationship closer to a ten.

_____

_____

_____

_____

Write in your journal or notebook to reflect on what you have learned or to repeat this process if you have more than two children.

Now, take the next step in the process and focus on the other parent in the picture.

Rate your relationship with your child's other parent on a scale from one to ten (ten meaning there is no room for improvement). Circle one:

I   2   3   4   5   6   7   8   9   10

Explain what it would take to move this relationship closer to a ten.

_____

_____

_____

_____

Now, take a moment to reflect on the process you just walked through. Start by reading over your responses. Reflect on your comments as a whole as well as any other observations you have made. Are there any common threads? Any patterns?

Lastly, take a moment and write down your thoughts regarding what all of this means. What do you need to do with what you have learned through this exercise?

_____

_____

_____

_____

EXTRA FOR EXPERTS!

If you are truly courageous—and truly want objective truth—ask your spouse or the other parent to rate your relationship with your child on the same one-to-ten scale. Then have them explain what they think it would take to move it closer to a ten.

Record what they said.

_____

_____

_____

_____

What did you discover? The implications are obvious, so I won't spend a great amount of time explaining all of the connections you either did or could have made. But essentially what you should walk away with is a clearer picture of exactly where you are in each of these relationships as well as an action plan for ways to improve each of these relationships. But most importantly, I hope you learned something about yourself and what you can do to bring these relationships closer to a ten.

I would even encourage you to look back at your lists and circle the items you wrote down that are specific to what you need to do. Some people even like to take a highlighter and highlight these items to help them jump off the page. I will tell you this, if something does not jump off that page, even just a little bit, then you are not being honest with yourself, which is the most important thing in any improvement or transformation process.

CONCLUSION

As we come to the end of section 3, "Spiritual Significance and Historical Context," I hope you can see that there is nothing going on now that has not happened to very powerful and anointed people who have gone before us. The difference is that you have their mistakes to learn from. You have a road map called the Bible to walk you through the land mines and traps that have so easily beset our predecessors. You also have your own personal history lessons to learn from through the activity you just participated in.

What's the point? Learn from the past. Take comfort in knowing that your God not only knows about this history lesson, but He has also provided very specific directions for how to parent in such a way that would bring life to your children, joy to your soul, and honor and glory to your heavenly Father. Learn the lessons of the past well. Move out with knowledge, wisdom, and power from on high, knowing yours is a just and noble cause. The battle has already been won at Calvary.

SECTION IV

PARENTING AT THE NEXT LEVEL

The miracle, or the power, that elevates the few is to be found in
their industry, application, and perseverance under the prompting
of a brave, determined spirit.[1]

MARK TWAIN

chapter 14

NEXT-LEVEL PARENTING DEFINED

Growth Principle #1:   No change without loss

Growth Principle #2:   No growth without pain[1]

—RICK WARREN

I HAVE DEVOTED MOST of my life to four pursuits—education, sports, the arts, and ministry—many times participating in all four at once. In the times I have devoted to these four pursuits, God has used each one to show me deeper truths about what separates success from failure, greatness from mediocrity, and God's will from man's efforts. In short, He has used these four pursuits to prepare me to write this book, as time and again God has given me glimpses of a life that is lived at the next level.

THE PHYSICAL WORLD

As I defined for you earlier, life lived at the next level is who we are when we are at our best. It is what is possible when we give ourselves completely to a cause. It is what we are capable of when we are trained, disciplined, and focused over an extended period of time.

In schooling, it is the high grade point average that is not just the result of higher IQs but rather the product of a disciplined study program, good teachers, tutoring when necessary, and daily devotion to a standard of excellence.

In music, it is what a person is capable of after many years of training, practice, devotion, and performance.

In ministry, it is what is possible when people are fervently praying, leaders are going above and beyond the call of duty, and spiritual priorities have greater weight than personal privacy and leisure.

In sports, it is what is possible when a team, or an individual, refuses to just "go through the motions" and instead gives himself or herself completely to a cause, not just for a contest or a race, but also during the many months that lead up to the event.

GAME SPEED

All through the 1990s I had the privilege of coaching football at one of the premier high schools in the nation. Over the course of ten years, we won more than one hundred games, five regional titles, one *Sports Illustrated* national championship, and two *USA Today* national championships. Those years, collectively, were full of extraordinary, life-changing experiences. I learned a great deal about coaching and playing at the next level. The simple truths I learned during those years parallel the same simple truths about a life that is lived at the next level as opposed to one where we just go through the motions.

The first lesson I learned came while watching our opponents warm up before games, week in and week out. I noticed that they warmed up and practiced at about half speed. I also watched as players either did not know or see the need to use the basic fundamentals as they went through their game-night preparation routine. They were only "going through the motions." In regards to doing anything more than that, they may have said, like many of you reading this now, "What's the big deal? It's only warm-ups." During the week, they may have said, "What's the big deal? Its only practice."

What these teams missed was the most important factor in being a success or a failure: you must practice at game speed using basic fundamentals, always, to develop game-speed *habits*.

I would watch the games week in and week out as opposing players would miss routine balls, slip and fall, miss blocks, or forget assignments because, when the game went to full speed, everything was new and nothing was familiar. Then, the worst part was hearing the coaches (through the walls at halftime or across the field during the game) yelling at the kids, telling them they "didn't want it bad enough" or that they "weren't giving their all." Neither was true. They simply had not practiced at game speed using basic fundamentals.

The second lesson I learned was that most games were not won or lost on any given Friday night. Most contests had been won months before the game even occurred because one team had committed a great deal more time to the cause, with far greater intensity in the off-season, than the other. The athletes were bigger, faster, and better trained and had spent substantially more time together in the off-season than the opponents. This resulted in a mismatch, not because of more talented athletes and not because of recruiting or an unfair advantage but because one team put in more time practicing the fundamentals in the months leading up to the season than the other did. It was enough to make a significant difference when the season actually rolled around.

The third fundamental lesson I learned was that many times we would beat more talented teams simply because we were more prepared. Our coaching staff put in more time, watched more films, and spent more time in planning and scheming than our opponents did, which resulted in victories over opponents with better athletes that we should not have been able to beat.

Do you see the application for parenting in the scenarios I detailed above? Just in case you missed it, here is a recap of the fatal flaws:

- *Going through the motions*: taking this brief season of life with your child for granted

- *Not practicing at game speed:* As a parent, this is when we are sloppy, lax, and inconsistent. Then, a situation occurs where we are expecting our children to act in a certain way, but they don't, and we are gravely disappointed. All that has happened is that our children did not react in the manner we expected, because we assume our thinking and reactions should automatically be theirs. The real problem is that we have not modeled, practiced, and reinforced this expectation consistently, so they drop the ball. The question is, though, who really dropped the ball?

- *Lax or inconsistent on the fundamentals:* Fundamentals are anything from rules and standards to traditions and nonnegotiables. When fences move, clarity is lost, resulting in mistakes that are made—some very costly.

- *Not committing to the planning process:* not developing a short-range and long-range intentional plan for developing your child in the character and priorities of Christ

- *Failure to have a game plan for the situations you will face as a parent:* It is the difference between being a proactive parent or a reactive parent. The difference is enormous, as are the results.

Parenting at the next level is not something that can be accomplished by an event, a trip, an afternoon, or an incredible moment. Parenting at the next level, just like the illustrations above represent, can only happen as the result of extraordinary effort, self-discipline, and going above and beyond the call of duty over an extended period of time. Most parents can commit to the moments, the trips, and the events, but they are losing the battle in the long haul.

I would like to show you in the pages that follow that it is not drudgery, and you are not required to give all that you can achieve, personally or professionally, to parent at the next level. Yes, there is sacrifice, and yes, it may demand a major overhaul of your priorities. But I believe with all my heart that the victory you will experience at the finish line will be worth every moment spent and every sacrifice made.

THE SPIRITUAL DIMENSION

All of the next-level components I mentioned above, in most situations, will result in effective parenting and great kids whether the parents are Christians or not. But, as you remember what we discussed before, and as you will read in the pages that follow, *raising great kids is not the goal.* In fact, if we are not careful, we will focus solely on the signs of a good kid and miss our God-given mission as parents entirely, which is to introduce our children to Jesus Christ and to move them toward a deeper faith and relationship with Him.

The first step in this battle for the souls of our children comes, once again, in realizing that there are two worlds that exist. True, next-level Christian parenting means placing as much focus and effort on addressing what is happening in the spiritual realm as you do in the physical realm. In fact, more is needed. I cannot begin to convey to you the level of intensity that is being exerted in that realm by all of the forces of evil to wrestle your child away from you and to lead them down a path away from faith in Jesus Christ. If I could find the words to say this in even stronger terms, I would.

Are you beginning to see the common threads of success?

- Extraordinary effort over an extended period of time
- Self-discipline
- Selflessness
- Planning
- Being teachable
- Having the ability to see and live life and all its experiences through the eyes of Christ

These are the hallmarks of next-level achievements.

I cannot begin to express how excited I am for you right now, wherever you are, whatever your situation. I am excited because if you are reading these pages, then you need to know that a team of people and I have been praying for you. I am excited because I do not believe things happen by chance or happenstance but rather by divine appointment. I am excited because I have seen what can happen when parents take this challenge and have personally witnessed families transformed as a result of parenting and living the way God intended.

I cannot wait for you to walk through the pages of each of the remaining chapters because I know the transforming truth that awaits you. I absolutely cannot wait for you to read section 6, "People of Joy With Children of Hope" because it will send you out with a mission and a purpose, and most importantly, with a vision of what could be.

So, for the next few weeks or so, get ready to get all the way in. Prayerfully read each remaining chapter, continue to have the courageous conversations you have heard about and will hear more about, and then purpose to be the parent God intended you to be. I know it can happen. Commit now to finishing the journey. God will do the rest.

chapter 15

PARENTING 101

The reason why Christians are so similar in their attitudes, values, and lifestyles to non-Christians is that they were not sufficiently challenged to *think and behave differently—radically differently* based on core spiritual perspectives—when they were children. Simply getting people to go to church regularly is not the key to becoming a mature Christian. Spiritual transformation requires a more extensive investment in *one's ability to interpret all life situations in spiritual terms.*[1]

—GEORGE BARNA

Y THOUGHTS GO back to the list of questions I put before you in a previous chapter. Have you had any of those conversations yet? They are so critical to this discussion that they must be more than a passing glance as you read through this book. *Do not assume you already know the answers.* Ask the tough questions, then listen and be open to the truth. Anyplace you choose to start must begin at the core of what is real and true. *Where are their affections? Where is their attention? Where is their imagination? Where is their focus?* If you will ask questions, listen intently, and simply pay attention to the comings and goings of their world, with God's help, you will discern the truth about your child.

STEP 1: TEACH THEM

Taking on the role of being "educator" to your child is clearly an admonishment from Scripture and is noted as the key to bridging the generational gaps of spiritual experience and divine intervention. If you are to break the chains of generational decline, you must teach your children who God is to you and who He can be to them. The first half of the Deuteronomy passage I spoke of earlier is very clear in its admonishment to parents. It says:

> Hear, O Israel: the LORD our God, the LORD is one. Love the LORD your God with all your heart and with all your soul and with all your strength. These commandments that I give you today are to be upon your hearts. Impress them on your children. Talk about them when you sit at home and when you walk along the road, when you lie down and when you get up. Tie them as symbols on your hands and bind them on your foreheads. Write them on the doorframes of your houses and on your gates.
>
> —DEUTERONOMY 6:4–9

Get the point? Does this sound like "going through the motions"? How can you do this, practically speaking, in your own home? Well, I asked some Christian parents this same question, and here is a sampling of their answers:

- Daily family devotions

- Mom or dad prayer time with the kids before bed

- Scripture memorization

- Framed words, scriptures placed strategically around the home

- Family sayings

These are very simple activities that will help you teach your child the ways of God. But please recognize that you cannot be lax. Making God the most important part of your child's life requires consistency and planning on your part. So step up! Be bold! Be victorious!

STEP 2: TELL THEM

> They will not see...they must be sought....They will not come, they must be brought....They will not learn, they must be taught.
>
> —AUTHOR UNKNOWN

What has God done in your life? Has He, in fact, saved you? How? When? Where? What did He save you from? How has He blessed you? How has He rescued you? Has anything ever happened that only He could have done? *Tell them.* Some of the most powerful testimonies that have come out of this book and my seminars are stories about when the parent shared their testimony with their child. I challenge you to tell them and then to give God the glory He deserves. This will give your child his or her godly heritage.

Tell them why you attend church each week faithfully and why your church life is so important. Tell them about this God you serve and why you, an intelligent person, choose to serve Him now. Pass up no opportunity to give God credit for anything in your life He deserves credit for. Look for ways to acknowledge His existence.

A passage in Psalms says it in a very powerful way. It says:

> Give ear, O my people, to my law: incline your ears to the words of my mouth. I will open my mouth in a parable: I will utter dark sayings of old: which we have heard and known, and our fathers have told us. *We will not hide them from their children, shewing to the generation to come the praises of the LORD, and his strength, and his wonderful works that he hath done.* For he established a testimony in Jacob, and

appointed a law in Israel, which he commanded our fathers, that they should make them known to their children:

That the generation to come might know them, even the children which should be born; who should arise and declare them to their children: that they might set their hope in God, and not forget the works of God, but keep his commandments: and might not be as their fathers, a stubborn and rebellious generation; a generation that set not their heart aright, and whose spirit was not stedfast with God.

—PSALMS 78:1–8, KJV, EMPHASIS ADDED

Why are we so private and secretive? Why are we so reserved about God's greatest gift to us? Embarrassment? Are we afraid of looking "uncool"? Who cares? Tell them! What an incredibly powerful admonition from the Scriptures for parents today. Tell them today, and then watch as the walls begin to come down. What you may find at the end of the day is that the walls were not of their making at all. You may discover that it was *you* with the bricks and mortar. It was *you* with all the reservations and protective mechanisms. Tell them and find out. Then write and tell me what you found.

STEP 3: PREPARE THEM

In discussions with parents at conferences or in one-on-one counseling situations, everything always comes back to this simple question: do you believe that there is an all-out war between the armies of God and the forces of evil for the minds, and ultimately the souls, of our children?

The cumulative effect of days upon years that we do not really understand is a subtle erosion. We come to doubt our place, we come to question God's intentions toward us, and we lose track of the most important things in life....We have forgotten that the heart is central. And we had no idea that we were born into a world at war.[2]

—JOHN ELDREDGE

Do you believe that there is an evil force that works night and day to influence and ultimately win the mind and imagination of your children? Or, is that just religious fanaticism and the ranting of an extremist? Because, quite frankly, if you answer no to the question asked above, then this book will not make much sense to you and will seem extreme at best, and fanatical at worst. I would only ask that if you are undecided, you allow me to make the case for an answer of yes to the question posed above, both from a biblical perspective as well as from a cultural perspective—then decide.

BIBLICAL COUNSEL

Scripture after scripture warns us that there is evil in the world and that we had better be on guard against the schemes and the attack of that age-old enemy, Satan, and his legions of angry, vengeful warriors. Probably the most recognizable and oft-quoted scripture on this topic of evil is found in Ephesians 6:10–12: "Finally, be strong in the Lord and in His mighty power. Put on the full armor of God so that you can take your stand against the devil's schemes. *For our struggle is not against flesh and blood*, but against the rulers, against the authorities, *against the powers of this dark world and against the spiritual forces in the heavenly realms*" (emphasis added). Second Corinthians 2:11 states, "…in order that Satan might not outwit us. For we are not unaware of His schemes."

In Mark 4:13, Christ tells the parable of the sower: "Then Jesus said to them, 'Don't you understand this parable? How then will you understand any parable? The farmer sows the word. Some people are like seed along the path, where the word is sown. *As soon as they hear it, Satan comes and takes away the word that was sown in them*'" (emphasis added).

THE PATH

I often wonder how many of our children's lives, especially our teens, are on the path that Mark refers to. I know so many Christian young people who, while they are in church every week and have asked Christ into their heart, their daily lives literally run on the path where so many of their unsaved friends travel. So many come and go, leaving their mark, their beliefs, their attitudes, and their morals on this path. If our young people take all of this in, the end of that path is hardened ground where once-soft soil used to reside.

You will rarely find a child who believes at the age of nine or ten that drinking alcohol is cool, especially if they come from a home where they are taught the opposite and their parents abstain. Yet the number of teenagers in this country who drink alcohol is astounding. The same can be said of drugs, sex, and every other destructive activity that the teens in this country seem to be engaging in by the thousands.

The obvious question I must pose is this: if it's not you who teach them that these things are bad for them, then who tells them that it's OK? Simply put, it is the well-worn path. Many Christian parents may not get to traverse this path very often that friends, teachers, and the media traverse daily, weekly, monthly, and yearly. What is discussed and decided on this path has enormous influence on our young people, churched and unchurched alike.

Concepts of right and wrong have been sown into the lives of our young people through the teachings of the Word. But when so much of their lives are spent with ungodly influences, or even just good kids who are unsaved, then these truths are taken away by Satan and replaced with lies and deception, relativism and situational ethics—hardened ground.

Am I saying that your children should never play with unsaved children? Of course not. Am I saying that your teen should never spend time with an unsaved teen? Of course not. But what I am saying is that if your child is going to spend a substantial amount of time with these friends, *you had better spend an equal amount of time tending the soil.* You must constantly cultivate the heart and work to counter the doctrine that is being taught and caught in the school of the real world.

Another reference, found in 2 Corinthians 11:14, says that Satan "masquerades as an angel of light." In other places throughout the Bible, Satan is referred to again and again as the deceiver, and for good cause. He comes in many disguises and forms and to the naked eye can be appealing and nonoffensive. But make no mistake, the end thereof leads to destruction.

Holy Scripture says:

> Be self-controlled and alert. Your enemy the devil prowls around *like a roaring lion looking for someone to devour.* Resist him, standing firm in your faith, because you know that your brothers throughout the world are undergoing the same kind of sufferings.
>
> —1 PETER 5:8–9, EMPHASIS ADDED

I would not hesitate to use the words *our children* when describing some of whom "your brothers" refers to. I would also be careful not to underestimate the term *devour* or pass it off as just a descriptor.

Lastly, the classic example worth taking a closer look at can be found in Matthew 4. Christ had spent forty days in the desert fasting when Satan came and tried to tempt Him. The Scriptures tell us, "He was hungry" (v. 2). Notice a simple fact: Satan tempted Christ where He was weakest at that moment, with the possibility of food. This is how it is with the deceiver. He knows where we are weak—*where our children are weak*—and that is where he lays the trap. Where is your child weak? You can bet that that is where he or she will be tempted. The place of weakness is where the attack will come.

THE CULTURAL WARS

> Those who live according to the flesh set their minds on the things of the flesh.... Those who are in the flesh cannot please God.
>
> —ROMANS 8:5, 8, NKJV

There is an all-out assault on our children today. Report after report is released yearly, and the findings of their studies on the entertainment industry and their continued pedaling of adult material to children and teenagers is overwhelming. These reports are a stinging indictment on the movie, music, and video-game industries. Basically, what the many reports indicate is that there is, and has been for some time now, a systematic, calculated effort on the part of all three industries to reach and market adult products to children. These reports specifically emphasize the targeting of young people for adult-level violence, sex, and in many cases pornography to our children. There can be no "right-wing extremist" conspiracies attached to these findings. Many of the findings come from independent secular agencies such as the Federal Trade Commission and most recently The RAND Corporation, a secular research organization based in Santa Monica, California.

In a recent study by the RAND Corporation titled "Watching Sex on Television Predicts Adolescent Initiation of Sexual Behavior," they found:

- Sexual content appears in 64 percent of all television programs, and those programs that contain sexual content average 4.4 scenes with sexually related material per hour.

- In the United States, 46 percent of high school students have had sexual intercourse.

- Each year in the United States, 1 case of a sexually transmitted disease (STD) is diagnosed for every 4 sexually active teens.

- The U.S. rate of teen pregnancy is among the highest of all industrialized countries.

- The average youth watches 3 hours of TV daily, and sexual messages are commonplace.

- Approximately 1 of every 7 programs includes a portrayal of sexual intercourse, depicted or strongly implied.

And here are a few of the clinchers:

- TV may create the illusion that sex is more central to daily life than it truly is and may promote sexual initiation as a result, a process known as media cultivation.

- Youths in the 90th percentile of TV sex viewing had a predicted probability of intercourse that was approximately double that of youths in the 10th percentile.

And here, in my humble opinion, is the saddest finding of all:

- Although intercourse among youths is common (46 percent), most sexually active teens say they wish they had waited longer to have sex.[3]

For you research buffs, these measures in the RAND study were based on a set of twenty-three programs using Nielsen ratings of the regularly scheduled primetime programs most watched by four groups (male and female twelve- to fourteen-year-olds and fifteen- to seventeen-year-olds), in the period from October 2000 to February 18, 2001 (the fall season up until the survey field period began).

It is my observation that a very interesting phenomenon is occurring in the television and motion-picture industries of America. It is my belief that the media in this country, especially television and film, no longer reflect the mood, moral direction, or daily life of the people who watch them. In fact, it is the opposite. Television and films are now being created to dictate the mood, create the morals, and influence the daily life of the people of this country. One example of this would be a recent article in the *USA Today* that found "about half of Americans over age 18 are married, but (only) 18.1 percent of major movie characters are."[4] Additionally, the number of sexual relationships outside the boundary of marriage is extremely high. Add to that the fact that we as Christians, while being an enormous percentage of the population in the United States, are basically absent from all television shows and movies, as is church attendance, prayer, and any consideration for spiritual discernment in decision making. Not only is this appalling, but it is also grossly inaccurate and completely *not* representative of the people in this country.

Over the last several years, we have had shows about teenagers—*The OC, Laguna Beach, That 70's Show, The Real World, Everwood, Dawson's Creek, Buffy the Vampire Slayer, Dark Angel, Popular,* and other *Beverly Hills, 90210* clones. In these shows, teenagers are being played by adult actors, in adult situations, with absolutely no regard for religion or a God that plays any kind of role in the decision-making processes, themes, or situations they encounter.

Worse yet, the parents are many times weak, unintelligent, and out of touch, therefore, the brunt of jokes and held in disdain. Many of the programs I have observed end with the parents seeing how wrong they were to have challenged their child and resolving that the child was right to go against their wishes.

It is so vitally important that you as parents and your church's youth leaders understand just how attractive this world is to our children. Even more than that, you must understand that in the world that is capturing their minds, Christians are not present. In fact, you and all you stand for are the "machine" they are told they must "rage against." It is a world where God is no more valued than a good-luck charm, a crystal ball, or an image of what they deem important based on how they interpret the world.

So now, we return to where we started in this chapter—the questions. Do you believe that there is an all-out war between the armies of God and the forces of evil for the minds, and ultimately the souls, of our children? Do you believe that there is an evil force that works night and day to influence and ultimately win the mind and imagination of our children? Or, is that just religious fanaticism? Is this just the ranting of an extremist?

To think it is anything less than a calculated, all-out assault would not only be unwise, but it would also be untrue. Make no mistake. The war is raging. You would be hard-pressed to find one single evangelical pastor in this country, and probably this planet, that does not think that the war for the souls of men and women, and especially the children in this generation, is raging with greater force now than at any other time in history. What will you do? To coin a phrase, it's your time on the edge.

> You need to overcome the tug of people against you as you reach for high goals....All men are afraid in battle. The coward is the one who lets his fear overcome his sense of duty.[5]
>
> —GEORGE PATTON

chapter 16

THE FULL ARMOR OF GOD

It is curious—curious that physical courage should be so
common in the world and moral courage so rare.[1]

—MARK TWAIN

BEFORE YOU GLANCE ahead and decide that this is going to be "just
another sermon" on the full armor of God, I challenge you to look
deeper. Spend a moment and walk through the exercise I have laid
out. I think you will find revelation and your purpose as a parent for today.

What an incredible admonition the rest of Ephesians 6 gives us when
it not only tells us what to be on the lookout for, but it also tells us what
we must do to stand when the battle is raging. It tells us what the "armor
of God" really is. *I always challenge parents to look at the items listed in Ephesians 6
and to identify exactly which of the pieces of armor their child does or does not possess.* It
is so critical to make this assessment because you can be certain that the
attacks our children will face will come at the points where there is insuf-
ficient defense. Read the last sentence that I have highlighted for you and
then reflect on it for a moment before going on.

Below, I have listed the armor of God. Take a moment to do the assessment for each of your children. My suggestion is that you *circle the ones you
know your child has and is prepared to use.* Then I would suggest that you go
through and *place a star next to the items that your child does not possess.*

The armor of God:

1. The belt of *truth*

2. The breastplate of *righteousness*

3. The *readiness* that comes from the *gospel of peace*

4. The shield of *faith*

5. The helmet of *salvation*

6. The sword of the Spirit, which is the *Word of God*

It then goes on to say that even with all of this, we should *"pray in the Spirit on all occasions with all kinds of prayers and requests. With this in mind, be alert* and *always keep on praying for all the saints"* (v. 18, emphasis added).

Once you have taken this inventory, begin to work and pray for the Lord to grant you wisdom as you endeavor to instill or install the items you starred. But before you launch out into the teaching or instilling and installing stage, ask the Lord to show you all that you must see and know as you embark on this educational adventure. For example, what exactly does the readiness that comes from the gospel of peace really mean anyway? What does righteousness entail?

Pause right here for about ten minutes and reflect on this concept before continuing. As I have stated again and again, it is important that you know your child's strengths and weaknesses, hopes and fears, and that you begin to see what God sees. Then, you must begin the work of teaching, instilling, affirming, reinforcing, practicing, modifying, correcting, coaching, encouraging, and all the stuff that is good teaching and good parenting.

NOT JUST A DRESS REHEARSAL

You are probably thinking, "Dr. Rich, what it sounds like you are saying is that we must prepare our children for war." And my response would be, "Yes! That is precisely what I am asking you to prepare them for."

A great and wondrous sign appeared in heaven: a woman clothed with the sun, with the moon under her feet and a crown of twelve stars on her head. She was pregnant and cried out in pain as she was about to give birth. Then another sign appeared in heaven: an enormous red dragon with seven heads and ten horns and seven crowns on his heads...The dragon stood in front of the woman who was about to give birth, so that he might devour her child the moment it was born.

She gave birth to a son, a male child, who will rule all the nations with an iron scepter....And there was war in heaven. Michael and his angels fought against the dragon, and the dragon and his angels fought back. But he was not strong enough, and they lost their place in heaven....Then the dragon was enraged at the woman and went off to make war against the rest of her offspring—those who obey God's commandments and hold to the testimony of Jesus.

REVELATION 12:1 5, 7 8, 17

The verse above from Revelation 12 is not about a dress rehearsal or even boot camp. We barely have time for that. The enemy is at the door, waiting to take our lives and our children's futures. We cannot allow ourselves to be lulled to sleep by the world's apathetic lessons of how to parent in today's society.

The world is asking you to think about what college or university your child will attend so you will set your focus there. The world will tell you he or she is just a kid and this is a time of innocence and not to overanalyze everything. "Just chill out," they say in essence. The world will tell you that if you push too hard, you will only push your child away. The world will tell you that if it's not broken, then don't fix it. The world will tell you that it is your job to provide the things your child needs to survive and to be successful in the physical world. "Just leave all the spiritual stuff to God and the church."

That brings us right back to where we started—deceptions, lies, and disguises. These are all part of the smoke and mirrors. *Do not be deceived!*

See beneath the surface. Believe that the Lord took great pains to prepare you and to warn you about the battle that rages for the souls of men and women—and their children.

Do not slumber when so great an assault is taking place right down the hall from your bedroom. Do not shrink from your God-given responsibility to educate and prepare your child for what lies ahead. Do not be too proud or too naïve to think that this message is for somebody else's child. And absolutely *do not* think that your child is just one of millions of children throughout the world and therefore couldn't possibly be the target of Satan's schemes and deceptions. Nothing could be further from the truth. He knows your child's name, where your child lives, what your child values, what your child adores, what your child fears, and most importantly, where your child is weak.

And last but not least, don't be so foolish to think he would use only the front door to enter your home. Once again…*nothing* could be further from the truth.

chapter 17

PARENTING 201:
STANDING IN THE LIGHT

Superficiality is the curse of our age. The doctrine of instant
satisfaction is a primary spiritual problem. The desperate
need today is not for a greater number of intelligent people,
or gifted people, but for deep people.[1]

—RICHARD FOSTER

I WOULD LIKE TO devote this chapter to the discussion of two terms: evil
and darkness. First, lets take a look at the term *evil*. I want to forewarn
you that this chapter, by far, will be the most difficult chapter in the
book for you to come to terms with. But it is my hope that it will also be the
most thought provoking and challenging portion of the book that you read.
It is my hope that, at the least, this chapter will challenge you to expand your
mental borders, rethink your mental pictures, and reconnect the dots with a
new construct. I also want to encourage you by telling you that in my seminars, for many, this was the most eye-opening and practical experience
they had, and one that each remembers and thinks about for weeks after.

To make these concepts easier to grasp, I have broken them down into
four steps that will help you combat evil and enrich the spiritual lives of your
children: (1) Open your spiritual eyes, (2) just say no (more often), (3) be
vigilant, and (4) get all the way in.

STEP 1: OPEN YOUR SPIRITUAL EYES

What is evil? What does it look like? What does it sound like? What does it feel like? How would one define the term *evil*? When I speak to parent groups, this is one of the first questions I ask: what is evil? I always get a wide variety of answers, and most sound like scenes from horror or slasher movies. But many times the descriptions include the following:

- Demons or demonic beings

- Meanness

- Murderers

- Sinister places

- Radical extremists

- Death-related infatuations or obsessions

- Terrorism

Then, after we have looked at this a bit, I shock them by suggesting a very simple definition of evil. *Evil is anything that separates or comes between us and God.*

Now, take a moment, pause, and reflect on this definition. Would you agree? If that is the definition of evil, then our list of what would constitute evil takes on a whole new form. The list could look more like the following:

- The beach

- A sport

- A car

- Late nights

- Friends

- Boyfriends or girlfriends

- A song

- A favorite performer

- A favorite celebrity

- A class

- A professor or teacher

And the list goes on. Now, you are probably thinking that this sounds extreme. But before becoming completely put off with this concept, consider these questions: *If you were Satan, how would you disguise evil if your goal was to entice your child? How would you create separation between your child and Christ?*

Now, to take this a step further, please take a moment to prayerfully consider each question below, then write your response in the space provided. I think you will find the answers to be very revealing.

If Satan wanted to keep your child from church, how would he do it?

_____

_____

If Satan wanted to separate your child from you, how would he do it?

_____

_____

We must remember that throughout Scripture, Satan is referred to as the deceiver, beginning with the snake in the garden who first asked, "Did God really say, 'You must not eat from any tree in the garden'?" (Gen. 3:1). Then, after doubt had set in, he boldly announced, "You will not surely die" (v. 4). And the trap, with all of its eternal implications, was set.

In his book *The Problem of Evil,* Charles Colson says, "When we close our eyes to the human capacity for evil, we fail to build the moral boundaries needed to protect us from that evil."[2]

Here is another way to look at the topic. Relationships, events, places, coaches, and teachers/professors must have a way of drawing your child nearer to Christ. If they result in greater separation, then a decision needs to be made. Reflect on that thought for a moment, and then journal what comes to mind.

You may be asking, "What about evangelism?" or "What about my child's unsaved friends?" Those are excellent questions. But you understand and know your child well enough to know which situations provide opportunities for evangelism and discipleship and which ones will just result in greater separation from God and His people. Pray this through for every relationship and situation. The Lord will give you the discernment you need to make the right judgment and choice.

In the description of evil I have given you to consider, appearances go right out the window. In fact, appearances may be exposed for the distraction or diversion that they really are. They may only be there to mask a greater ploy at work that is designed to bring your guard down long enough to allow evil to take root. Sound extreme? Well, let's look at a few examples.

The magazines, newspapers, and talk shows are filled with stories of teens who fooled us all—teens who were thought to be safe, secure, wholesome, and trustworthy only to find out it was a sham, a masquerade, and a lie we had all fallen for. The truth is only discovered as a result of the tragic consequences of a life lost, a family torn apart, or a childhood stolen.

One biblical example came to mind right away. It takes place first in Joshua 23, where Joshua delivers his parting comments to the leaders of the chosen nation of Israel:

> The LORD your God himself will drive them out of your way. He will push them out before you, and you will take possession of their land, as the LORD your God promised you. Be very strong; be careful to obey all that is written in the Book of the Law of Moses, without turning aside to the right or to the left. Do not associate with these nations that remain among you; do not invoke the names of their gods or swear by them. You must not serve them or bow down to them. But you are to hold fast to the LORD your God, as you have until now.

The LORD has driven out before you great and powerful nations; to this day no one has been able to withstand you. One of you routs a thousand, because the LORD your God fights for you, just as he promised. So be very careful to love the LORD your God. *But if you turn away and ally yourselves with the survivors of these nations that remain among you and if you intermarry with them and associate with them, then you may be sure that the LORD your God will no longer drive out these nations before you. Instead they will become snares and traps for you, whips on your backs and thorns in your eyes, until you perish from this good land, which the LORD your God has given you."*

—JOSHUA 23:5–13, EMPHASIS ADDED

Then, sure enough in the Book of Judges, not long after Joshua was dead, the people thought they could have it both ways. They thought that God would surely honor mercy, but they found out that all God truly wanted was obedience.

It seems that then, just as now, every man does what is right in his own eyes. This seems innocent enough until you read in Judges that it is only a short amount of time until the men are now worshiping the gods of the foreign women and in doing so have betrayed their God and brought great judgment upon their nation.

Joshua...died at the age of a hundred and ten....After that whole generation had been gathered to their fathers, *another generation grew up,* who knew neither the LORD nor what he had done for Israel. Then the Israelites did evil in the eyes of the LORD and served the Baals. They forsook the LORD, the God of their fathers, who had brought them out of Egypt. They followed and worshiped various gods of the peoples around them. They provoked the LORD to anger because they forsook him and served Baal and the Ashtoreths. In his anger against Israel the LORD handed them over to raiders who plundered them. He sold them to their enemies all around, whom they were no longer able to resist. Whenever Israel went out to fight, the hand of the LORD was against them to defeat them, just as he had sworn to them. They were in great distress.

—JUDGES 2:8, 10–15, EMPHASIS ADDED

God had given what seemed a barbaric command to the Israelites when they came into the Promised Land. He told them in no uncertain words to destroy everything, the idols, false gods, and people—all of them. But the next generation did what seemed right in their own eyes, and no longer followed the God of Joshua and Caleb. The result was devastating, and in the end, rather than enjoying the land God had given to them, they became slaves to the very ones they had been told by God to destroy.

Why do we always think we are smarter and wiser than God? They saw these beautiful foreign women and could not see the harm in getting to know them better. They fell in love (or lust) and the next thing you know, the lives of God's people are so intertwined with those of the pagan culture that one could not tell the difference between the two. But God could and did. Our God, who is a jealous God, had to once again deal ever so harshly with His children. But sadly, for many it was too late. They had crossed over, never to return to their God, never to receive His promise and blessing.

Anything that separates us from God, anything that comes between us and our God, must be seen for what it is—evil.

DARKNESS AND LIGHT

Let's look at a second term, *darkness*. How would you define *darkness*? Well, the list usually looks something like this:

- Demons
- Vampires
- Serial killers
- Satan
- Witchcraft

- Sorcery

- Terrorists

I would like to offer a very simple definition of *darkness* that really sets the stage for the key to success with our children in this great battle. Darkness means, simply, *an absence of light*.

Even a nonbelieving scientist would be hard-pressed to refute this definition of darkness. Now, this being so, it also stands to reason that the further away from the light source we venture, the greater the darkness. Because it is so essential that you are able to connect the words associated with darkness, I have constructed a visual picture of what the effects are of being in or out of the light. In the lists below, the light represents God's perfect will for a person's life. Darkness, on the other hand, represents places where there is less and less light the further one walks away from the light.

I ask parents and students at conferences to tell me the characteristics of *spiritual darkness* as opposed to when a person is living and operating within the lighted area or in God's will. The lists go something like this:

Darkness	Light
Frustration	Clarity
Anger	Vision
Confusion	Safety
Can't see clearly	Security
Can't see at all	Healthy
Guessing	Hopeful
Lost	Aware
Impetuous	Patient
Worry	Peace

Darkness Effects	Light Effects
Wrecklessness	Boldness
Blindness	Faith
Regret	Hope
Hardness/cynical/sarcastic/overly critical	Love
Harmful or painful consequences	Provision
Panic	Salvation
Addiction to whatever makes the darkness feel better	Healthy relationships
Repeated mistakes	Victory
Bitterness	Joy

Do you remember playing hide-and-seek in your neighborhood as a child? When we would play, the streetlight was always the "free spot." But you will also remember that the further from the streetlight, the darker it was, and the harder it was to see where your friends were hiding. This is also the perfect word picture for the kind of darkness and light I am describing. It would look something like that old streetlight.

DARKNESS AND LIGHT ILLUSTRATED

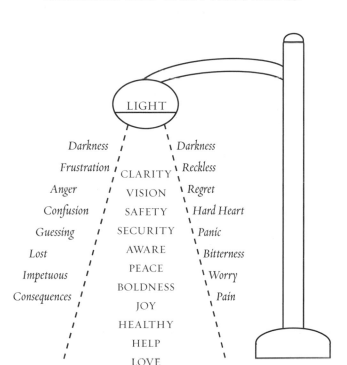

MAKE THE CONNECTION

Take a moment to study the lists and examine the picture. As you examine the comparison, the test is this, try to perceive which lists best describe your child. Perhaps there are qualities on both sides of the lists that could describe your child. The point is simple: *the more your child stands in the center of the light, the more the things on the light list will come to describe your child, and vice versa.*

STEP 2: JUST SAY NO (MORE OFTEN)

Darkness can manifest itself in your child's life in a variety of ways, because wherever your children go and Christ is not present in that place, then there is an absence of light. Of course, your child takes with him or her a measure of light that comes in the form of the Holy Spirit. But as a parent, you need to be vigilant in protecting your child's light so that it will not be overcome by greater darkness. You have prayed for wisdom and guidance from the Lord, and based on the questions you have answered above and in previous chapters, you are aware of the areas of your child's greatest weakness. It is your duty to have discernment about things that could affect or snuff out the light your child has, so in order to protect them, you may have to limit the places they go, the people they interact with, and the things they watch or listen to. Here are a few examples/scenarios to trigger awareness:

- Your child spends the night or regularly spends time at an unsaved friend's house. Every time your child walks through those doors, he or she is entering a place where there is an absence of light.

- Your child gets in their own car or in a car with a friend and spends many hours over the course of a week driving around listening to music that is degrading, violent, dark, and promotes immoral behavior, then they are constantly in a place where there is an absence of light.

- Your child retreats to their room for hours on end, spending countless hours on the phone or the Internet with friends who do not know the Lord. They are spending their time in a place where there is an absence of light.

- Your child goes to one or two movies per week or month. You know that most of these movies will not represent a Christian lifestyle or even an acknowledgement of God in the script. Then, for three to four hours per week or month your child will be watching and enjoying the lives of characters and situations that exist where there is an absence of light.

- Your child attends school several hours per day. Every time their non-Christian teacher strays from academic content and ventures into areas of social or political relevance, then your child could be hearing and learning a worldview where there is an absence of light.

I am not saying that our children should avoid all of these things mentioned above and that all of these things are evil. What I am hoping you will do is not take one single moment of your child's life for granted. Don't you live in the dark about the people and activities your child spends time with. Turn on the light. Have honest discussions. Listen to them. Do your research. Tend the soil.

STEP 3: BE VIGILANT

Darkness cannot drive out darkness; only light can do that.[3]
—MARTIN LUTHER KING JR.

Most of the scenarios I described above involving your child's friends, teachers, music, and entertainment have a belief system of their own. They are not issue- or belief-neutral. This means that not only in many of these cases is there an absence of light, but there is also the presence of the enemy. Therefore, you must not send your child into a building where the enemy lies in wait without first preparing them for what lies ahead. If they are not prepared to handle what lies behind that door, then consider keeping them from walking into a slaughter. This just seems reasonable to me.

We are losing kids *every day* in this battle, and there is a line a mile long of parents who would love to speak to you about the doors they wish they had kept their children from entering until they were better prepared. So be vigilant now so that you won't have the same regrets.

Many a great and mighty man of God has fallen throughout history. This does not even take into account the hundreds and thousands of those who fell in complete anonymity in the neighborhoods all around us.

Here are a few facts to consider:

- More than 7 million adolescents drank at least once in the past year.

- Almost 3 million teens drank alcohol about once a month or more in the past year.

- One million youths drank at least once a week or more in the past year.[4]

- Underage drinking accounts for 11 percent of all alcohol consumption in the United States.[5]

- Of the 14.6 million teen-aged marijuana users in 2002, approximately 4.8 million used it on twenty or more days in any given month.

- Each year, 100,000 teens are treated for marijuana dependence.[6]

- An estimated 1.8 million (0.8 percent) of youth aged twelve and older are current users of cocaine.[7]

- Suicide is the third leading cause of death among people between the ages of fourteen and twenty-five.[8]

We have a nation of children screaming to be heard by a nation of parents who choose not to listen with spiritual ears. Oh, we will tell them we are all ears, but we hear what we want to hear and see what we want to see, and so many times what we see is the façade, the lie, the deception.

STEP 4: GET ALL THE WAY IN

Many times, I think we are all guilty of refusing to use our spiritual eyes to see evil or to acknowledge darkness because that could possibly mean confrontation. It could cost us a meal each week in fasting. It could mean having to get out of bed in the middle of the night to pray when prompted.

It could mean disrupting a very harmonious house where there is peace and quiet—but no real *peace*.

It could, and will, definitely mean paying attention at a time when there is so much vying for your attention. It could mean personal sacrifice. It could mean coming home from work when you can and not sticking around at work, finding things to do to avoid going home. It could mean any number of things for each parent. But make no mistake: if you are to truly make a difference in the life of your children, it will not come without cost and sacrifice. You must get all the way in.

What is that cost for *you*? What must *you* do to begin this process? I think *you* already know a few things you must do differently. I truly believe that as you read this book, the Holy Spirit will convict and show you the things you must do to move forward in this battle. But amidst all of the sacrifice and challenges you undertake as a parent, the greatest transformation that must take place is the one within yourself. In his timeless book *My Utmost for His Highest*, Oswald Chambers says, "The measure of the worth of our public activity for God is the private profound communion we have with Him."9

Your measure as a parent in this battle will be marked by "the private profound communion" you have with your Lord and Savior Jesus Christ. The real battle lies here deep inside the heart of the parent, the one God entrusted with His creation—your child. Once again, the challenge is there. You must get all the way in. Now, turn the page and continue the journey. The next step is the most important step you will take.

chapter 18

PARENTING 301: THE "ME" FACTOR

We received His blessings and know His Word, *but do we know Him?*

—OSWALD CHAMBERS, EMPHASIS ADDED

OR EVERY BEAUTIFUL flower, piece of fruit, or towering tree, there are three key elements that are necessary for survival. But when all three are working together, there is strong growth and incredible life-giving results. The three essential parts are the *root system*, the *environment* that the plant must live in, and the *portion of the plant we all see.*

Parents are the root system for their children. The children, of course, represent the actual flower, piece of fruit, or towering tree. The *environment* is the place in which the plant (or child) must live. The number of object lessons is endless, but there are a few that I really want to emphasize here. First, the strength or weakness of any plant form is determined by the strength and integrity of the root system. Second, as powerful as the root system is, the plant has no control whatsoever over the environment where the plant must live. Third, while the root has no control over the environment, it certainly must be stronger in its support and attachment to the plant in harsh environments.

Simply put, the strength of the root, more often than not, literally determines the type of life the actual plant will have, including longevity, health, and beauty. Deep stuff!

Do you know what will shape your child the most over the span of their life, and especially in their growing-up years? Relationships, and even more importantly, their relationship with Mom and Dad.

DADS

- Did you know that a *son's view of his father* and his relationship with his father will many times *determine his view of God*?

- Did you know that your son's work ethic, courage, mettle, and security all stem from his interactions with you?

- Did you know that your children gauge what they think they are capable of in life by *your* personal accomplishments, thus their love for your old stories?

- Did you know your child's concept of *respect for authority* will based on their relationship with you?

- Did you know that *your daughter's view of you will be your daughter's view of men* in general and in relationships specifically?

- Did you know that the most significant relationship your daughter will ever have, or not have, is with *you*?

- Did you know that your daughter's sense of *worth, security, approval, and confidence* will all directly or indirectly stem from her relationship with you?

- Did you know that your daughter needs physical affection and *one-on-one personal attention* and that if they do not receive it from you, they will find it elsewhere?

Many psychologists believe that all romantic relationships that occur in a girl's life will be positively or negatively affected by the way she interacts with her dad. A good father will leave his imprint on his daughter for the rest of her life.

To those of us who bear the name "Dad," I cannot impress upon you enough how imperative it is that we show our affection. Many a young woman who opts for immoral sexual relationships does so because she can scarcely remember a time when her father so much as touched her. Unaffectionate dads, without ever wishing to do so, can trigger a daughter's promiscuity. All this leads me to write with a great deal of passion. Dads...don't hold back your affection...and don't stop once they reach adolescence. They long for your affirmation and appreciation. They will love you for it.[2]

—CHARLES SWINDOLL

MOMS

- Did you know that your daughter's sense of *empathy, perseverance, and her nuances* all come primarily from you?

- Did you know that there is no greater honor for you as a mother than for your grown daughter to someday call you *her best friend?*

- Did you know that your son's sense of *tenderness, gentleness, and affection* will come from what he learns from his interactions with you?

- Did you know that your son's *number one need from you is respect* and that a boy, or a man for that matter, seeks that respect through what he does, such as his job, sports, music, academics, hobbies, or other areas of personal interest or activities?

- Moms, did you know that the way you train your son to treat you *will determine the way he treats his future spouse?*

Parents

- Did you know the number one fear of teens in America is that something bad may happen to their family, and more specifically, the loss of a family member through death or divorce? This is followed closely by the next two greatest fears, which have to do with not getting the right education and not being able to make it financially without you. Bottom line, you are the anchor, and you are the source of stability, security, and hope in a world that is increasingly hostile to people of faith, and our kids have figured that out. And based on what they see all around them, the thought of losing you or not having you when they need you is a major point of concern and stress for today's teens.[3]

- A simple Google search for the number one cause of stress in people will reveal a myriad of topics, each dependent on what it is that they want to sell you or cause you to believe. But even amidst a plethora of causes listed, there is one common thread—*change*. Whether it's the economy, national security, or the environment, *change* is the operative word. It is no different for your teen. While their issues may not be your hot-button issues, change is still the catalyst for a myriad of emotions and reactions and has to be considered when trying to figure out root causes for behavior and emotions.

- Did you know that the greatest need of children from their parents is *affirmation*?

- Did you know that one of the most important duties you have for the kingdom of Christ is to instill a *godly heritage* deep within their hearts?

- Did you know that the number one reason kids give for not trying drugs is fear of disappointing their parents?[4]

THE BIG TWELVE

What are the twelve most important things you and your spouse can do for your children every day?

1. *Grow strong together*, as husband and wife, in the Lord.

2. Model and give healthy love and *physical affection*.

3. Affirm, encourage, and *listen* to your children. (The number one complaint of children about their parents is that we don't listen to them.)

4. Teach your children to have a *Christian worldview* that includes an eternal perspective.

5. Establish and maintain *family traditions, rituals, and reminders* (photo albums and the like).

6. Model and develop in each child a *personal prayer life*, teaching your children that they truly can talk to God.

7. Instill in each child a respect and love for *God's Word*.

8. *Keep your promises.*

9. As much as is possible, *build daily routine* into your children's lives.

10. *Admit* when you are wrong, and say you are sorry.

11. As a family, be active participants in your faith community, both at *church* and in your social lives.

12. *Enjoy your children, and let them enjoy you.*

Do you realize that you are the root system for your offspring? For you to think that you can have all of the strength you will need without specialized planning and care for the long haul would be foolish at best and tragic at worst. Can you see the need to commit to spiritual growth and that it is essential for you to continue to grow in depth and in breadth? You must grow in your relationship with God, His people, and in relationship with your children if you are to parent at the next level.

THE LIVING WATER PRINCIPLE

One of the best word pictures for the power of a parent as it relates to this "root system" concept is found first in Psalms and then is personalized in the Gospel of John.

> Blessed is the man who does not walk in the counsel of the wicked or stand in the way of sinners or sit in the seat of mockers. *But his delight is in the law of the LORD, and on his law he meditates day and night. He is like a tree planted by streams of water, which yields its fruit in season and whose leaf does not wither. Whatever he does prospers.*
>
> —PSALM 1:1–3, EMPHASIS ADDED

> Whoever believes in me, as the Scripture has said, streams of living water will flow from within him. By this he meant the Spirit.
>
> —JOHN 7:38–39

What an incredibly powerful admonition from Scripture for parents today. Did you catch it? There is a distinct spiritual concept taught in these two scriptures that emphasizes just how powerful your influence can be. I call this the living water principle. Have you ever noticed the amount of vegetation that grows nearest bodies of water? I lived most of my life in Southern California where there are many regions that are just vast areas of dry desert. But even in the worst conditions possible, where there are bodies of water such as rivers, streams, or the like, there is vegetation that flourishes along the banks.

That is the point precisely. You see, *your proximity to the life source—the living water—will determine your spiritual health.* But this is even bigger than that. God gives us all something called free will, and in that, He allows us to plant ourselves wherever we want. Oh, sure, He tells us again and again in Scripture to draw near to Him or to remain in Him, but ultimately, He lets us decide how close to the life-giving water we choose to live.

Now, here is the clincher, until our children are old enough to make the decision for themselves about where they will plant themselves, *you* are that source of life-giving water. *You* are the well that they are planted next to. *You* are literally responsible for the water that feeds the root system, just like the water on Earth does the same for trees and vegetation that grows next to it.

The goal is simple. You must plant yourself in the center of His will, learn from His Word, grow in your relationship with Him, deepen, and mature so that out of *you* will flow rivers of living water, just like it says in the Gospel of John. That is how powerful this concept is. That is how important it is for you to be firmly established and planted. Drawing near to your Lord and Savior Jesus Christ is the most important thing you can do as a parent.

Are you beginning to get the picture? We cannot wing it. We absolutely cannot settle for just going through the motions. There is too much at stake.

Let me ask you a couple more personal questions. *Are you teachable?* Are you willing for God to do whatever He has to do to get you where He wants you to be spiritually?

God's Holy Scripture says this about the ability to be taught and molded by God and learning to see with spiritually discerning eyes:

> The man without the Spirit does not accept the things that come from the Spirit of God, for they are foolishness to him, and he cannot understand them, *because they are spiritually discerned.* The spiritual man makes judgments about all things, but he himself is not subject to any man's judgment.
>
> —1 CORINTHIANS 2:14–15, EMPHASIS ADDED

Come unto me, all ye that labour and are heavy laden, and I will give you rest. Take my yoke upon you, and learn of me; for I am meek

139

and lowly in heart: and ye shall find rest unto your souls. For my yoke is easy, and my burden is light.

—MATTHEW 11:28–30, KJV

Those who live according to the sinful nature have their minds set on what that nature desires; but *those who live in accordance with the Spirit have their minds set on what the Spirit desires.* The mind of sinful man is death, but the mind controlled by the Spirit is life and peace.... You, however, are controlled not by the sinful nature but by the Spirit, if the Spirit of God lives in you.

—ROMANS 8:5–6, 9, EMPHASIS ADDED

Since, then, you have been raised with Christ, *set your hearts on things above,* where Christ is seated at the right hand of God. Set your minds on things above, not on earthly things. For you died, and *your life is now hidden with Christ in God.*

COLOSSIANS 3:1–3, EMPHASIS ADDED

Take a moment to think about the things we talked about today. Think especially about the living water principle and what that means to you. What will you do with this new knowledge? Where are you planted? Are you planted in a place that will allow His living water to flow through you? Think on these things, and then spend a minute in quiet reflection.

The next section of this book, section 5, "Declare Your Intentions," will deal with ways to live out the living water principle. But please take heart in knowing that the journey does not come without great reward and blessing. The victory that lies ahead has already been won. The battle you will fight is a righteous one. The greatest thrill of all is knowing that Christ stands at your side and His precious Holy Spirit is there to guide and protect you every step along the way. While this path is fraught with danger and uncertainty for most, those whose hearts are stayed on Christ will find this journey to be a great honor, blessed hope, and certain victory.

SECTION V

DECLARE YOUR INTENTIONS

Do you want to know who you are? Don't ask. Act!
Action will delineate and define you.[1]

THOMAS JEFFERSON

chapter 19

PREPARE YOUR HEART

Nothing shapes your life more than the commitments you choose to make. Your commitments can develop you or they can destroy you, but either way, they will define you. Tell me what you are committed to, and I'll tell you what you will be in twenty years. We become whatever we are committed to.[1]

—RICK WARREN

CROCKETT JR HIGH SCHOOL
LIBRARY
ODESSA, TEXAS

Y FRIEND, IF you have truly walked through the journey in this book, I want to personally affirm you and your commitment to your children. But before this section of the book is complete, I will be asking you to do two things. First, I will challenge you with one task, and second, I will ask you to complete one statement. The task, just like the statement, is something that only you can complete. No one else can do it for you, and there is no pat answer.

The task I will challenge you to complete is to simply *declare your intentions*. The statement I will be asking you to complete is, "As for me and my house…" (You fill in the blank.) What will be your legacy? What will you be remembered for when all is said and done? What is your credo?

Time after time in the Old Testament, when God's people entered a new territory, or were blessed by God in some way, they paused to do a few things. First, they stopped to construct an altar or to give an offering of some kind to their God in gratitude for all He had done. Second, God's people would gather stones to create a monument that would be a reminder for all generations to come of the commitment they had made on that day to their God. In both scenarios, this was no simple, casual event but rather a bold proclamation for all to see. It also served as a visual accountability marker to remind themselves, and the generations to come, of the magnitude of the event on that day.

Really, they were no different than we are today in many regards. They knew that as the emotion drained and the days began to fill up with the "stuff" of life, it would be easy to let time lessen the importance of the commitment made. This book, if you are not intentional about who you plan to be in the days and years ahead, will result in the same minimized impact as the emotion drains and the "stuff" of life begins to kick in. If you are not intentional about taking action for your kids' sake, time will lessen the impact of what you have experienced these last several days and weeks.

With that being said, stop right now and thoughtfully answer the following questions:

What has the Lord spoken to you throughout the course of reading this book?

_____

_____

Where has He convicted you?

_____

_____

What has He told you to do?

_____

_____

Has He called you to a higher level of commitment? What is that commitment?

_____

_____

How can you and I walk this earth and not recognize that we owe our very coming and going, our breath, and our life to God? How can we not come into full submission and service to our King—our closest friend? Everything you have read to this point is of absolutely no use, no worth, and no help whatsoever without the most important factor that must come into play—His power! And I know of no place where the access to that power, that infilling of the Holy Spirit, is greater than on our knees.

> I have been driven many times to my knees by the overwhelming conviction that I had nowhere to go. My own wisdom, and that of all about me, seemed insufficient for the day.[2]
>
> —ABRAHAM LINCOLN

That is where the first step toward parenting at the next level must begin. It is where every God-ordained revolution ever began, every righteous battle was forged, and every ounce of forgiveness was ever felt—on bended knee, figuratively or literally, in humble submission and contrition before a just, righteous, loving, forgiving, all-powerful, all-knowing, ever-present, victorious God.

Find some time today to stop to pray—on bended knee—a very personal prayer of thanks and gratitude. Then spend a moment or two in quiet reflection as you listen to what God says to you.

chapter 20

TRUTH AND CONSEQUENCES

There are dimensions of our glorious King that will never be revealed to the casual, disinterested worshiper. There are walls of intercession that will never be scaled by dispassionate religious service. But when you take steps to break out of the ordinary and worship Him as He deserves, you will begin to see facets of His being you never knew existed. He will begin to share secrets with you about Himself, His plans, His desires for you. When you worship God as He deserves, He is magnified.[1]

—JENTEZEN FRANKLIN

E PHESIANS CHAPTER 4 holds an incredible passage of pure truth related to truth and consequences. It says:

It was he who gave some to be apostles, some to be prophets, some to be evangelists, and some to be pastors and teachers, to prepare God's people for works of service, *so that the body of Christ may be built up* until we all reach unity in the faith and *in the knowledge of the Son of God* and *become mature, attaining to the whole measure of the fullness of Christ.*

Then we will no longer be infants, tossed back and forth by the waves, and blown here and there by every wind of teaching and by the cunning and craftiness of men in their deceitful scheming. Instead, speaking the truth in love, *we will in all things grow up into him*

147

who is the Head, that is, Christ. From him the whole body, joined and *held together by every supporting ligament,* grows and builds itself up in love, as each part does its work.

—EPHESIANS 4:11–16, EMPHASIS ADDED

One Sunday service, my pastor gave a visual illustration of what this passage means and the implications it has for today's Christian. He placed a small box about the size of a shoebox on top of the pulpit. He explained that for a believer to simply attend church weekly, while separating himself or herself from the rest of the body in lifestyle and geography, it would be like taking your hand and severing it from your arm and placing it in a box. Now, the body would heal, find a way to manage without the hand, and then continue to grow and mature into adulthood. Meanwhile, the severed hand would not continue to grow or be useful to the rest of the body. It would live the rest of its existence in an isolated, lifeless state of decay. Powerful stuff!

Please do not miss what I am saying here because it goes to the heart of what this section, "Declare Your Intentions," is all about. The only way you will ever develop, grow, and mature in your faith is through relationship with other believers (fellowship), through studying God's Word (discipleship), and through committing your time and resources to your God (service). You must do one of the most difficult tasks for many people (especially men)—you must *commit.* You must grow deeper. You must mature. Otherwise, you are building your house on sand—quicksand even. Your heartfelt commitments made here today won't last or stand the test of time. Words and the emotion of the moment will not draw you closer to your Savior, no matter how many tears you shed during a worship service. And sooner or later someone in the church is going to offend you, step on your toes, sit in your seat, or even lovingly rebuke you. What will you do? Who will you be in that moment?

Sunday mornings, if not taken with a steady diet of fellowship, discipleship, and service, will accomplish little more than a constant diet of candy bars and chocolate. It will not sustain life.

In a little while, I am going to be asking you to get on your knees before your God and to declare your intentions. But no matter how powerful that moment may be, and I believe it will be a defining moment, without getting all the way in, it will be like you had nothing more than a chocolate bar for breakfast. You will still feel empty a few hours later, and *no matter how many more you eat, it will not sustain life.*

> People do not live by bread alone, but by every word that comes from the mouth of God.
>
> —MATTHEW 4:4, NLT

THE SIN FACTOR

I believe some of you who are reading this right now have fallen. You have fallen, and the weight of your sin is enormous. You are crushed and do not feel the least bit worthy of God's attention or His time. I have good news. Scripture says:

> The LORD is close to the brokenhearted; he rescues those whose spirits are crushed.
>
> —PSALM 34:18, NLT

Scripture also declares that He is faithful and just to forgive (1 John 1:9). He is a merciful God who died to set you free so that you would forever be free from the chains of your past.

One of the most gifted leaders in the church today, Darlene Zschech of Hillsong Music Australia, does not come bearing a sword or a shield but rather with a song and a praise on her lips. In her insightful book *Extravagant Worship* she says this:

> The name of Jesus pulls down walls. Do you actually believe that God can smash walls in your life? I do. He has done it to me time and time again. I've personally seen my own walls of insecurity,

pride, mistrust, fear....I've watched God dismantle these walls as
I've praised Him regardless![2]

Get up! Confess it, repent, seek His mercy and grace, and go before Him
and let Him wash you in His blood and forgive you. He will give you a hope,
a promise, and a future. (See Jeremiah 29:11.) Then be changed, recom-
mitted, and resolved to parent and live at the next level. But whatever you
do, do not stay where you are. Get up, and get connected.

> God has given us his Spirit. That's why we don't think the same way
> that the people of this world think.
>
> —I CORINTHIANS 2:12, CEV

Now, I am about to explain something to you that I believe is incredibly
critical to the rest of your life in Christ. When we sin, we set into motion a
series of events and consequences that, if unchecked, can destroy our ability
to function as godly parents or as children of God. We all fall short of the
glory of God daily. Scripture tells us we sin all the day long. Though we do
not set out to do so each day, it is still almost inevitable that we will miss the
mark—and often. But here is what you *must* grasp: sin creates separation, and
separation, if unchecked and not dealt with, will lead to isolation. Now, here
is the implication for you, specifically, as a parent: When we isolate, we do
what experts refer to as *"disconnect."* It is this disconnect that occurs between
parents and children that results in devastating and tragic consequences in
families all across the nation, especially in the church of America.

It is absolutely critical that when you fall, big or small, you stop immediately upon sensing the conviction of the Holy Spirit and deal with the sin.
Confess it, repent of it, ask for God's forgiveness with a truly contrite heart,
and then get up and continue on believing God's promise to forgive and
restore you. If you struggle with a sin that you continually fall prey to, you
must seek out an accountability partner who can help hold you accountable
weekly or even daily if necessary. This kind of sin is called a "besetting sin."

Whatever you do, do *not* underestimate the ability of sin's negative effects on you as a parent and as a child of God. *Christ did not die so you could live a life separated and disconnected from those you love most.* He came to die so that daily you can be reconciled, restored, forgiven, and loved. Don't miss this.

WORSHIP LEADER—RONNIE

Ronnie was and is to this day a very talented, charismatic person just oozing with personality, gifts, and a passion for the Lord. Throughout most of his life, Ronnie has been involved in music at some level. As an adult, he had shucked the trappings of this world to be a musician full-time. Ronnie had it all—the voice of an angel, musical ability, and a great music-filled job in the entertainment industry.

While his dream to be a rock star never quite materialized, Ronnie eventually married, had two wonderful daughters, and began using his gifts more and more for the Lord. Ronnie became very involved in the worship community at a large church, eventually becoming one of the main worship leaders each Sunday morning.

But Ronnie had a few minor character flaws that were keeping him from all the Lord had for Him, and it took a discerning leadership team at this large church to actually take a stand and challenge Ronnie in a way that could have either led to improving the inner man or caused him to walk away indignant, discouraged, and wounded.

Each year, every member of the worship community (choirs and special groups) could try out to be one of the up-front worship team members, which was quite an honor in a church as large as this church was. As part of the try-out process, potential worship leaders had to fill out forms, write out their testimonies, and submit other minor documents all by a certain date.

Well, Ronnie wasn't so hot with deadlines, being places on time, or just dealing with details in general. So when the forms were due, Ronnie's weren't there. They ended up only being a day or so late, but when he went to turn them in, he was promptly told that it was too late. Ronnie turned on the charm and explained his excuse, but it was to no avail. The leader held his ground. Ronnie would have to wait until next year to try out again—try out again for a position that had been his for two years.

Ronnie was hurt, offended, indignant, and every other word you might imagine he would be. And while he may not have recognized it at the time, he was at a fork in the road, and what he would do with what just happened would determine his entire future.

What was he going to do? He was, after all, more talented than the singers who took his place. All of his closest friends were the ones on those worship teams. His whole identity was gone. Ronnie was disillusioned. Who wouldn't be?

It was at this time that Ronnie made the most important decision of his life. Rather than wallow in his misery or take his family and go somewhere where his gifts and talents would be appreciated (which he considered strongly), he instead decided to give up his right to himself and instead just focus on his children and his family. What happened next is extraordinary.

One Sunday, he took the next step of faith, and, even though wounded still, he went to the children's pastor and volunteered to help in his kid's Sunday morning programs, not having any idea what he might be asked to do.

But one Sunday they had him lead worship with the children, and he loved it! Better yet, they loved him. He had no idea the joy he would receive from doing that until he actually did it one Sunday morning. Here's the great part! Guess who became the children's worship pastor just a few months later? That's right—Ronnie! He has even produced a few children's worship CDs and now tours the country as a children's worship leader and performer.

What a miracle! God honored his obedience and submission. Yes, it was painful. Yes, it hurt. Yes, everything in him was telling him to walk away and go where he was appreciated. But instead, he learned the most valuable lessons of all. He learned that God does honor those who are committed to the details and that when God closes a door, He knows what He is doing. We can either strive with man or surrender to our God. Praise God that he made the right decision.

> But the people blessed by God must persevere no matter what. They must understand that Satan fights the hardest when the greatest spiritual breakthroughs and blessings are just around the corner. Yet, even as the Christ child in Bethlehem was rescued from what seemed to be certain doom, so God will protect and nurture his chosen people.[3]
>
> —JIM CYMBALA

It goes without saying, then, that the more we know God, the more we will have His thoughts, His eyes, His ears, and His perspective. Anything less is flying spiritually blind.

chapter 21

THE REST OF THE STORY

God's...gracious Word can make you into what he wants you
to be and give you everything you could possibly need.

—ACTS 20:32, THE MESSAGE

Only one life to live, and it soon will pass, and only what is
done with God will last.[1]

—HENRY BLACKABY

DID YOU SEE yourself anywhere in the scenarios that played out
in the last chapter? Are you growing? Are you spending time in
fellowship with other believers? Are you in a small group? Are you
giving faithfully of your time and your resources? Are you growing in your
faith? Are you responding to God's hand of guidance, or are you resisting
and taking the wheel declaring, "I'll drive"?

I know this is an overused analogy, but there is wisdom behind even such
simple things as the instructions flight attendants give you just before take-
off. They tell you that when the oxygen mask drops down in an emergency
situation, place the oxygen mask on yourself before placing the mask on your
child. Although this would defy every natural parental instinct we have,
there is really great wisdom in doing this in the order they suggest.

But this is the secret to parenting at the next level. You must take your
personal faith to the next level first, then bring your child along. That is
the greatest truth I could tell you. It is absolutely essential. *You must grow*

deeper. This must be your most important priority. And here is why this is so critical.

You can parent to the absolute best of your ability and do every modern technique known to mankind. You can follow your child everywhere they go, making sure they never fall down, get hurt, or come anywhere near danger. You can even pick their friends and arrange play days with only the best children from the best families. You can be supermom or superdad and spend every waking moment devoted to your children—*and still fail.* But the man or woman of God should have one goal as a parent: that they would develop the mind of Christ.

Let that sink in for a moment. Your most important task as a parent to your child is to move them into a place where they can develop the mind of Christ, because you won't be able to see everything your child does, but you should be able to see what God sees.

> My thoughts are not your thoughts, nor are your ways My ways....For as the heavens are higher than the earth, so are My ways higher than your ways, and My thoughts than your thoughts.
>
> —ISAIAH 55:8–9, NKJV

Our aim should not be to hear every word or thought that comes from our child's mouth but rather *to hear what God hears.* Our goal should not be to feel proud of our child's many accomplishments and accolades but to feel and sense about your child *what Christ feels and senses.* To truly parent at the next level, your personal quest must be a very personal and spiritual commitment to develop the mind of Christ. Please believe me when I tell you that it will not only change the way you parent and the way you live, but it will also radically alter your life.

> Let God transform you inwardly by a complete change of your mind. Then you will be able to know the will of God—what is good and is pleasing to him and is perfect.
>
> —ROMANS 12:2, GNT

For my doctoral dissertation, the title of my study was *Common Parenting Practices and Strategies of Parents of Very Successful High School Seniors.*[2] What I had to do first was to determine what "very successful" meant, which I accomplished through interviewing a panel of experts. Criteria were items such as high GPA, attendance records, discipline records, sports team captains, club presidents, and other indicators. The panel determined that if a child possessed five of seven indicators, then they would be considered a "very successful high school senior."

After we determined who this very elite population was (which ended up being the top 3–5 percent in each school) in three different high schools in three different cities, they were given a survey to take home to their parents. The parents then filled out the survey regarding their parenting practices and strategies from when their children went from birth to age five, elementary age, middle school age, and high school age. Another element of the survey I added was a survey that told me about the parents themselves. Remarkably, the biggest finding of the study was that the most common characteristics about these kids' upbringing weren't the things their parents did, because that varied quite a bit. What was most common were the characteristics and life accomplishments of the parents. The parents in the study had these things in common:

- They knew their children intimately.

- They gave attention to detail in their children's lives.

- They made a conscience effort to be present in the home.

- Their children were their highest priority.

- The parents of these children were committed to ongoing personal development: nearly all were high school graduates, had higher levels of post–high school education, and 75 percent of all these parents were college graduates.

This was astounding, but God is not surprised. It should be the greatest news that I could give you. The single biggest factor in parenting at the next level is the one thing you can control, the one person you can change—YOU!

YOUR RELATIONSHIPS MATTER

I want to tell you as plainly and as emphatically as I possibly can that you can get down on your knees today and be more committed than ever. You could even read your Bible every morning and pray over your children every night. But if you—mom or dad—do not get connected on a weekly basis with other believers in a relational setting, you will fail. And even worse than that—you will fall. *Count on it!* It is just a matter of time.

To believe that you can fully connect with God while living in a state of "disconnect" with other Christians, is to believe a lie. I am not talking about seasons of life where God takes us and separates us out for a time to do a work in us. Of course God does that from time to time. But what I am taking about is a lifestyle, a yearlong existence that is rich and full of relationships with other Christians. That is where true growth is nurtured and you are sharpened, cared for, and loved.

If you are to truly take on the mind of Christ, you must connect with other believers and allow yourself to be loved, listened to, cared for, challenged, rebuked, influenced, and encouraged by godly men and women on a regular basis. They must know your name and be allowed to spend time beneath the surface of your protective outer layer of defenses.

Scripture also talks about the strength that can be found in relationship with other believers:

> Two are better than one, because they have a good return for their work: If one falls down, his friend can help him up. But pity the man who falls and has no one to help him up! Also, if two lie down together, they will keep warm. But how can one keep warm alone?

Though one may be overpowered, two can defend themselves. *A cord of three strands is not quickly broken.*

—ECCLESIASTES 4:9–12, EMPHASIS ADDED

I will take it a step further than that and say this: it is in relating to and spending time with others the way I described earlier that helps you mature as a person. How are you maturing? You are maturing through relationships. And here is the clincher: I believe with all my heart that the degree to which you are able to broaden your understanding of relationships and are able to connect and communicate with others will be the same degree you will be able to connect with and communicate with your God.

Relationship is not innate, and it is not instinctual. *It is learned.* If this were not true, then thousands of marriage counselors would be out of business. There is absolutely no way to learn how to have a successful relationship with Christ sitting in a large crowd of people on a Sunday morning once a week, even if you went every week for five years. You must take the next step and begin to connect, and the next step may literally be taking a walk over to your church's information booth and asking about ways to connect and to get involved. Whether it is through getting involved in a ministry at your church or simply committing to be a part of a small group, take that critical first step and begin to connect in relationship this week.

These are just suggestions. I know that whatever church you go to, there are many ways for you to get the kind of support you need to go to the next level. Pick one, and then commit.

GET ALL THE WAY IN

God cannot give us happiness and peace apart from Himself, because it is not there. There is no such thing.[3]

—C. S. LEWIS

There it is, all spelled out in the previous pages. Who are you going to be? Right now is your appointed time of decision, and I am compelled to challenge you right now to declare your intentions. As God said in 1 Kings:

> Then it shall be, if you heed all that I command you, walk in My ways, and do what is right in My sight, to keep My statutes and My commandments, as My servant David did, then I will be with you and build for you an enduring house, as I built for David.
>
> —1 Kings 11:38, nkjv

Won't you come before your Father, your creator, your best friend, and lay your life at His feet today? Won't you commit right now to being all He created you to be? Won't you surrender your right to yourself and take up your cross and follow Him? Declare it. Give it. Surrender it all to Him, then watch what a beautiful thing He creates out of your simple act of obedience and surrender.

> *Now what I am commanding you today is not too difficult for you or beyond your reach.* It is not up in heaven, so that you have to ask, "Who will ascend into heaven to get it and proclaim it to us so we may obey it?" Nor is it beyond the sea, so that you have to ask, "Who will cross the sea to get it and proclaim it to us so we may obey it?" No, the word is very near you; it is in your mouth and in your heart so you may obey it.
>
> *See, I set before you today life and prosperity, death and destruction.* For I command you today to love the Lord your God, to walk in his ways, and to keep his commands, decrees and laws; then you will live and increase, and the Lord your God will bless you in the land you are entering to possess....
>
> *This day I call heaven and earth as witnesses against you that I have set before you life and death, blessings and curses. Now choose life, so that you and your children may live and that you may love the Lord your God, listen to his voice, and hold fast to him.*
>
> —Deuteronomy 30:11–16, 19–20, emphasis added

Following a time of prayer, take a moment in the space provided to reflect on all the Lord is showing you right now. Spend some time in prayer and reflection about what God is speaking to you about this very moment. Take your time and be thorough, knowing that these may well be words that you will come back and read in the days and years to come. These could possibly be the words your child reads years from now as they look back at your life and the decisions you chose to make.

_____

_____

_____

_____

_____

_____

_____

_____

_____

_____

_____

_____

In this next chapter, I will walk you through a commitment time that I think will serve as a defining moment in your life as a parent.

chapter 22

AS FOR ME AND MY HOUSE...

I will show you what he is like who comes to me and hears my words and puts them into practice. He is like a man building a house, who dug down deep and laid the foundation on rock. When a flood came, the torrent struck that house but could not shake it, because it was well built. But the one who hears my words and does not put them into practice is like a man who built a house on the ground without a foundation. The moment the torrent struck that house, it collapsed and its destruction was complete.

—LUKE 6:47–49

FOR THE NEXT fifteen to twenty minutes, I want you to find a place where you will not be interrupted. Be sure to have something to write with and to write on. Here is what I want you to do:

First, I want you to humbly come before your God in prayer and worship and just spend a moment acknowledging that He is your God and you are His child. This is your act of worship. Henry Blackaby describes worship like this:

Worship is a deliberate, steady, focused time with God. Worship anticipates not only an encounter with God, but also a clear next word from God. Out of worship comes a clearer and more focused relationship of faith and obedience with God.[1]

Powerful stuff. Take just a moment to lift Him up and acknowledge Him as your God.

Second, I want you to take some time to just thank Him for all He has brought you through. Begin with your salvation experience, your life since that day, all that you own, and all He has provided for you.

Third, spend a moment or however long it takes to thank God for your family. Pray a prayer of acknowledgment for the qualities and gifts He has placed in each member, and the way each member responds to you.

Now, the focus shifts to you. I want you to ask God three questions, pausing after each question to listen and to let God fill your mind with His thoughts concerning each question.

- *Question 1:* Lord, what needs to change in my life for me to be the Christian I need to be? What do I need to do to get all the way in?

- *Question 2:* Lord, what needs to change in my life or lifestyle for me to be able to be the mom or dad You would have me to be?

- *Question 3:* Lord, who do I need to go to, as soon as possible, to ask forgiveness?

Through establishing what I call your life's credo statement, I believe that you will experience a profound, defining moment before God. So in the space provided, I would like for you to complete the sentence I have given you. This may take you a moment to think about, or it may just come flooding out of your heart like a tidal wave. But either way, what you write will be your statement to God and a defining moment.

MY CREDO:

As for me and my house, to that end, I purpose to:

_____

_____

_____

Congratulations! You have just crossed over a line that separates you from most of the parents in this country. You have examined your life, looked long and hard at what God would have you do with His gift to you, and declared your intentions. Now take a moment to once again come before God with a thankful, fearful, sincere heart, and ask Him to walk with you through the journey that lies ahead. He promises to never leave you or forsake you. He will be there every step of the way. Come before Him, and make that connection with a grateful heart in humility and gratitude, and express your love for God. It only gets better and better from here.

When finished with this profound, life-changing time of prayer and commitment, take a break. Rest up a bit and allow the fullness of what just happened to sink in. And believe me when I tell you this, even if you go out from this moment and one of your kids acts up, your spouse is insensitive about something, or you make a mistake of some kind, it's OK! You are on the right path, and your process of leaving a legacy is a process that will prove itself a worthy pursuit over the next weeks, months, and years. It will happen! You will experience the joy of your salvation, and you will see victory when and where it matters most! God's Word declares it, I have seen it, and you will know it!

With that said, once you have rested a bit and regrouped, turn the page and finish the journey in this book. The best is yet to come. I want to show you in section 6 all that could be. I want you to see the possibilities that are there for the taking for those who call themselves "people of joy with children of hope"!

SECTION VI

PEOPLE OF JOY WITH CHILDREN OF HOPE

The question is not whether we will be extremists, but what
kind of extremists we will be....The nation and the world
are in dire need of creative extremists.[1]

MARTIN LUTHER KING JR.

chapter 23

LEAVE A LEGACY

P ARENTS LOVE TO play the "what if?" game when thinking about the futures of their children. We focus on all the things they need to do to be successful at this or that. But if we have learned anything in the last several chapters, it should be that we *must* begin to see our children through His eyes. We must develop a greater sensitivity to God's presence and to His leading.

> By wisdom a house is built, and through understanding it is established; through knowledge its rooms are filled *with rare and beautiful treasures.*
>
> —PROVERBS 24:3–4, EMPHASIS ADDED

In the last chapter, we said that our goal should be to develop the mind of Christ so that we might have eyes to see what He sees. This includes the future. That's right, just when you thought it was safe to go back in the water, I tell you that this whole parenting at the next level includes our children's futures as well. *Ouch!* You may be thinking, "But we have that all figured out already. We don't need God's help with that one."

WHAT'S GOD UP TO WITH YOUR CHILD?

I want to take a moment to walk you through an activity that I believe will reveal a very profound fact about each of your children. I am going to ask you a question, and it is a question that will undoubtedly have a different answer for each of your children. What is unique about your child? By *unique*, I am talking about notable qualities—something that they just exude. Answer that question for each of your children. I have given you an example using three of my own daughters. The answers for each of them would look like this:

Child	Qualities	Gifts
#1	A true worshiper Independent Enthusiastic Passionate A doer	Music and dance Does not need other's approval An encourager One hundred percent effort in what she values Loves to work with her hands
#2	Sweet and gentle A faithful friend Relationship driven Accepting of all Loves babies and young children Fearless	Very loving and compassionate Trusted friend, loyal/committed Will spend hours with one or two friends, working out their problems Sees injustice, senses hurt, and acts on it Nurturing Trusts authority without question

Child	Qualities	Gifts
#3	Adventuresome Sense of humor, loves to laugh Very athletic Fearless on the field Intuitive/perceptive	Foods, athletics, activities, friends, places Loves to laugh and entertain, lighthearted Very gifted runner, competitive A thinker and a listener
#4	Sense of humor Loving/a cuddler A pleaser A reader Fearless Adventuresome Independent Lover of people Love of learning	Humor Competitive Quick learner Leader

Get the idea? Think carefully and intentionally about each child you have, take a moment to do this activity, and then record your answers in the space I have provided. Do this before you turn to the next page, because on the next page I want to show you something that I think is very profound. So don't spoil it. Do the work first, then turn the page and read on.

Child	Qualities	Gifts

Did you do it? Isn't it an awesome experience to pause to reflect on the significance of each child? Now here is the clincher. This may be hard to grasp for some of you, while others of you may have figured this out long ago. All those plans you have for your child, all those worries you have about whether they will get into the right college or score high enough on the SATs or ACTs, and all the other things you do daily to help your child toward the goals you have set for their lives—those are good goals, worthy goals even. But all those things are what *you* are doing in the life of your child. Not to say that those things aren't important, because I know for many of you, they are. But what I want to show you is this: the things you listed in the chart above are extremely significant indicators for what God is doing in the life of your child.

Think about that for a moment. God has built into every life, every precious soul, a plan and a purpose. He has looked into the womb and, Scripture says, literally knit together every life with a specific design in mind, a design to fulfill His purpose here on Earth. But even more extraordinary than that, for me at least, is that He knit each child together in a way that brings Him pleasure. All of those qualities you listed were for a purpose, yes, but they were also given to enhance and create opportunities for fellowship with God. What an incredible thought.

Now the tough part…Go back and look over the list of qualities and gifts you listed for each child on the previous page. Put on your "imagination cap" for a moment and think of all that God could do with the qualities and gifts He instilled in each child. Imagine what could take place if each of the qualities were to be yielded to God for His purposes. Look especially at each gift, and imagine what could happen if that gift were totally and wholly dedicated to God and His purposes on Earth. Can you see it?

It is very hard, as a parent, to shut off the career, financial-needs, and quality-of-life buttons that we all have in our minds. In fact, we don't even turn it on. It just comes on every time we think about the future. It just illuminates all by itself, every time we try to picture our children as happy, productive adults. We just want the best for our children. But somewhere along the way, some of us seem to have excluded God's provision, God's plan, or God's mission on Earth as an option listed under our definition of *best*. We have placed God in very comfortable places, such as Sundays, retreats, camps, the Bible, and prayer.

Now, just to clarify, I am not suggesting that every child surrender to the mission field or the pastorate, but I am suggesting that our children must view God's direction for their lives and the gifts He gives to go in that direction, as a way to serve Him, be it in official ministry, their secular workplace, or their personal lives.

The question for you is very simple. Are you willing to let God be God? Take a moment to journal about the gifts and skills you see that are unique to each of your children, and what those could mean for the kingdom. Dream big; hold loosely.

_____

_____

_____

_____

_____

_____

_____

_____

_____

_____

_____

_____

_____

chapter 24

WHAT IF?

Every generation needs a new revolution.[1]

—THOMAS JEFFERSON

CROCKETT JR HIGH SCHOOL
LIBRARY
ODESSA, TEXAS

I WANT TO WALK you through a "what if" exercise a good friend of mine once walked me through. He said that we have a tendency to see our children on this side of their future. By "this side," he meant on this side of what could eventually happen. But God has an entirely different perspective. God sees our children on the other side. He sees who they will become. He knows how the story turns out. He knows the plans He has for them.

> I am God, there is no other; I am God, and there is none like me. *I make known the end from the beginning,* from ancient times, what is still to come. *I say: My purpose will stand, and I will do all that I please... What I have said, that will I bring about;* what I have planned, that will I do.
>
> —ISAIAH 46:9–11, EMPHASIS ADDED

Have you ever watched a movie you have already seen or a replay of a ball game when you already know how the story or the game turns out? It is an extraordinary thing to watch, especially with the ball games. You see the coach of the winning team worry, yell, get angry, and look perplexed. You can just see his stomach in knots. But *you* know it is going to turn out OK, so you don't have that anxiety. You know how it turns out for the losing coach as well, and you watch them to see how they will respond to the adversity coming their way.

Here is the "what if" game I would like for you to play. I want you to get a mental picture of one of your children. You know their strengths, but you know their weaknesses too. You know your hopes, but you also know your fears for that child. Now, I want you to picture this. What if the child you are picturing right now was to grow up and find the cure for cancer? What if that child would be the first to walk on Mars? What if your child were to be the one to find a miracle cure for AIDS? What if that child was the next Billy Graham or Beth Moore. What if thousands of people would come to Christ through the life of your child? What if your daughter was going to write the most incredible worship songs of her generation, as Darlene Zschech has done in hers? What if your child was to win a Nobel Peace Prize? What if you knew today that one of these was to be true for your child?

Well, what if you knew? *How would you look at your child today?* What would matter? What would you do differently? How would you treat them? How would you prepare them? How proud would you be of them, even though they have yet to have achieved their finest hour? *What would be different?*

I really believe that if we are to truly parent at the next level, we must see our children from God's perspective, the same God that knit them together in the mother's womb, each with an extraordinary purpose and mission. Is there a higher call than to be all that God created you to be? Is there a greater end than that? If we are to see what God sees, from His perspective, then we must focus on who they are becoming and where they are going. We must do as I have told parents for more than fifteen years: *begin with the end in mind.*

Let's go back now to your list of character qualities and gifts. Your job in the development of these areas is to nurture, encourage, and provide opportunities for that child to exercise their gifts.

NURTURE

To nurture a gift or a quality, you simply have to acknowledge it when it is displayed, encourage it when it is performed, and affirm it as from the Lord. Tell them what you see, and even more importantly, tell them what God sees. Tell them they are gifted in those areas. Children love to hear about themselves, and they love even more to be complimented and affirmed. Remember, especially with boys, that their number one need is respect, and they get this through affirmation of what they do. See the good, affirm it, and build on it.

ENCOURAGE

At first glance, you would think that encourage and nurture are very similar, but they really are not. Child psychologists stay busy year-round working with children with little or no self-esteem. Children, by nature are not generally social risk takers. And often criticism and even good, constructive advice or parental coaching can drive a wedge between an attempt and quitting.

When it comes to activities, be quick to encourage and slow to correct, coach, or criticize. Remember that very few of us in this life are naturally gifted at things, but all of us can become good at anything with enough practice, instruction, and time.

PROVIDE OPPORTUNITIES TO EXPERIMENT WITH IDENTITY

This is the tough one because it usually means sacrifice, time, and resources. It is where terms like "soccer mom" and "taxicab parents" come from. I hear a lot of pastors preaching less activity and less involvement for children these days. I know that many times we can be overzealous in this area, and it can mean sacrificing family time. But I do believe that, to the extent your children can participate without eliminating family and church time, you should encourage and provide opportunities for your child to participate in as much that matches what God is doing in their lives as possible.

What I would really encourage you to do is to plan your child's activity calendar around specific purposes. I know no place that is better to start than the lists of character qualities and gifts you listed earlier. And, yes, that could mean the activities for each child could be different. Not every child is going to be a concert pianist, athlete, cheerleader, swimmer, or an *anything*. It may be easier for you to drop and shop if they are all at the same place at the same time, but this really isn't supposed to be about you.

Now you are mad at me. Now I'm in your kitchen and you don't want me there. But remember, this was never about being normal. This was never about going through the motions. This was never about just getting them through to a good job, a nice home, and the American dream. This has been, from page one, about an extraordinary life for a chosen generation with extraordinary results.

Do you believe that? Do you believe that there is a great movement of God in our nation right now? Do you believe that your child is part of a generation of believers that will radically change the world in the last days? Do you believe that God will tarry much longer? Do you believe that God has an incredibly important purpose and mission in this world for your child like no other generation before? I do! I absolutely do.

Oh, parents, the war is raging. It is raging all around us in the heavenly realms, in the spirit world, and your children are at the center of the storm. That is the message I have been sent to say to my generation. I say it as passionately as I possibly can. But I am also sent to say that victory is ours, if we will only get all the way in. Do you believe there is a battle raging for the hearts and minds of the next generation? Do you really and truly know your child? Do you understand that this is not a new battle but an age-old confrontation between good and evil, darkness and light? Will you commit to parent at the next level, regardless of the personal sacrifice that might mean for you? And will you get all the way in? And lastly, do you understand that the battle was won at Calvary? Do you grasp the significance of the power, wisdom, and victory that are yours for the taking if you will simply surrender your will and your life to the leading of the Holy Spirit? Are you ready to live life and parent at the next level?

chapter 25

BEGIN WITH THE END IN MIND

In the end, it's not the years in your life that count, it's the life
in your years...Always bear in mind that your own resolution
to succeed is more important than any other.[1]

—ABRAHAM LINCOLN

I GREW UP IN a small town about sixty miles northeast of Los Angeles,
California. I say a small town, but I mean small by Southern California standards, as there were approximately forty thousand people.
But what I remember most about my childhood is the games my dad would
take me to at the local high school. In our area, there were three high schools,
and each was considered a rival of the others.

Every week, whether it was basketball season or football season, I would
read the papers to know every fact I could gather about the local teams,
especially the school that would be my high school someday. I dreamed of
playing varsity sports there someday and having my picture in the paper. As
the years went by, my time to shine was drawing ever nearer. When it finally
came my time to go to high school, I was ready. It was great.

I did everything I ever dreamed of and made my parents very proud. I
lettered in three sports, had my picture in the paper regularly, and in our high
school of three thousand students, I was at the center of everything there was
to do. I went to all the dances, played the sports, had tons of friends, and was

one of the big men on campus. I loved high school. It is probably why I have loved working with high school students even to this day.

But I have to tell you, as honestly as I possibly can, that at no time in my seventeen plus years had I ever given two minutes of thought to what came after high school. It was always something way out there. My focus, dreams, and ambitions were all limited to high school. Sure, I knew everything there was to know about pro football and baseball, but when I graduated from high school, guess what? Those were not an option.

What followed were three of the most difficult years of my life. I was not big enough or fast enough for a college scholarship. While my GPA was 3.0, the universities were not beating down my door to get me to come. All I had ever known was sports, church, and school. I was a lost soul (so to speak) without any idea of what I would do next.

I decided to enroll at the local community college and take the basic college transfer courses until I could figure out what to do with the rest of my life. I almost did not make it. Those were very dark and lonely days for me, and guess what? I found out early on that the folks in college did not give a rip about my athletic prowess in high school. Every identity I had in high school, short of my faith, was gone.

Now, I obviously recovered and went on to figure a thing or two about what I should do with the next sixty years or so of my life, but I learned a very valuable parenting lesson through all of this that I absolutely need to pass on to you. In the 1990s, I spent ten years working on the campus of a parochial high school. I immediately made a connection to those post–high school experiences I went through when I saw an entire high school full of students whose focus from day one was on college and beyond. And it literally determined every step they took leading up to graduation and beyond. They had figured it out. They understood the concept of awareness and preparing for life beyond high school. Guess what the only type of sweatshirts they were allowed to wear at school? College sweatshirts. They all had their favorite college teams and mascots and were avid fans.

A Matter of Focus

It's not all about setting your child's expectations on college early, although that may be part of it. The message is much bigger than that. The point I want to make to you is that their focus will be where your focus is. What my father said was important was what I thought was important. And what you set out there in your child's future to look at will enter their filter as important and a focus point.

My challenge to you is this. Are their kingdom places or goals that you could be setting out there as focus points, or are they all just physical world "go to college and get a good job" kind of stuff? Short-term missions projects are in higher demand and being utilized by churches more than at any other time in the church's history. Is a religious vocation even an option?

What about the kind of college your child will attend? Are you at the least making your child aware of the different options that are available including Christian colleges and universities?

Begin with the end in mind. Know that their focus will be where you place it. It will be as wide open or as limited as you will take the time to present. Don't just leave it all up to the school to take care of it for you. You have to remember that the natural tendency of a teenager is the point of least resistance, followed closely by a second fact of teenage life: procrastination is an art form. And lastly, the clincher being the assumption that somebody will take care of it for them or make them do it when it has to be done.

Begin with the end in mind. By *begin*, I mean that you must mentally go out to the end of your time with your child and see them as an adult. Then ask yourself, "What can I do now to place an awareness in them for the things they will need to know or be able to do when I am not there to do it for them." A scary thought, I know, but a necessary one if you believe you truly do have a say regarding their windows of opportunity and life choices. I am living proof that you absolutely do.

chapter 26

WHAT'S LEFT TO DO?

In many parts of contemporary culture, it is acceptable to believe in God, but only if you keep your belief in a private box. Yet Christianity will not remain privatized. It is not merely a personal belief. It is the truth about all reality. Christians must learn how to break out of the box, to penetrate environments hostile to our faith, make people see the dilemma they themselves face, and then show them why the Christian worldview is the only rational answer.[1]

—CHARLES COLSON

I WANT YOU TO know how excited I am for you to have reached this point in the journey. God will truly bless you and honor you for your commitment to this process. I have just two more things for you to do. One is to recognize what you have left to do and the other is to answer, reflectively, a very important question. These actions will serve as the road map for you to navigate the rest of the years God gives you with your children. No small thing. Let's get started.

The first thing I would like for you to do is to list the qualities and character traits you want your children to leave home with and to enter adulthood possessing. These should reflect all of the things life will be throwing at them—all the loss, success, tragedy, joy, times of plenty and times of want, disappointment, and hope they will surely encounter.

Reflect on the gravity of this question, and then do your best to list your response. (Do not feel obligated to fill every slot, or to be limited by them either.)

List the qualities and character traits that you want your child to leave home with when they leave the nest:

1. _____

2. _____

3. _____

4. _____

5. _____

6. _____

7. _____

8. _____

9. _____

10. _____

11. _____

12. _____

13. _____

14. _____

15. _____

Now I am going to ask you to do three things:

1. I would like for you to go through and underline all of the qualities and character traits that your child can define accurately and completely. Michael Josephson is the founder and president of the now-famous Josephson Institute of Ethics, which then created the widely used

Character Counts character education program, used in schools all across the nation. A key element of this program is called the TAME method. T stands for teach, A stands for Advocate, and M stands for Model. But the one I want to focus on is the T for Teach. What they found is what parents have been overlooking for years, and that is that we cannot assume that children can accurately define critical character terms as simple as honesty, fairness, and compassion. They are not "caught," and must instead be "taught," and therefore is the first letter in the TAME method.[2]

2. I want you to place an asterisk (*) by the ones that your child possesses right now. By "possesses," I mean they understand this and they live it in their lives.

3. I want you to circle the ones that your child does not possess yet or display in his or her life consistently.

Here is your task from this day until they leave the nest:

- The ones you could not underline, you must teach.

- The ones you circled are your focus for prayer, instruction, correction, and observation.

- The ones you placed an asterisk by need to be affirmed every time you see evidence.

As you can see, this is simple rubber-meets-the-road kind of stuff. Now, let me make it just a little bit more focused and accurate. I need you to rewrite the list of qualities and character traits again here below in the space I have provided. It will only take a second, but I am about to show you one last critical piece of information.

Rewrite the qualities and character traits from the previous page and list them here:

1. _____
2. _____
3. _____
4. _____
5. _____
6. _____
7. _____
8. _____
9. _____
10. _____
11. _____
12. _____
13. _____
14. _____
15. _____

The next thing I am going to ask you to do is simply write the following words next to each quality or character trait: *without me.*

After you have done this, go ahead and read them aloud, adding the words *without me.* It isn't just that they are able to do these things, but rather that they can do these things or possess these qualities without you being there to help them or, better yet, make them. Get the point? This is what you must accomplish in the time you have left. Do you see how important this is? To help you see how important this is, try to figure out which qualities and traits on your list they could just do without. Are there any? Probably not.

I have found the process you just walked through to be an excellent exercise to do with kids. Show them your list above, and find out how many they can actually define. Start there. Then instill, teach, instill some more, model, instill, and affirm. You can get there, but it will require focused attention on something, or someone, worthy of it.

chapter 27

THE MILLION-DOLLAR QUESTION

Then it will be, that if you listen to all that I command you and walk in My ways, and do what is right in My sight by observing My statutes and My commandments, as My servant David did, then I will be with you and build you an enduring house as I built for David, and I will give Israel to you.

—1 KINGS 11:38, NAS

BEFORE WE END our journey together, we both need to engage in one final activity that I think is an incredible place to finish this journey…for now. So go ahead and put your "imagination cap" back on and imagine yourself getting up from where you sit. Now take a walk with me.

THE WALK ACROSS THE FINISH LINE

Let's take a walk out to the end of this thing called life as we know it here on Earth. Now sit back down with your chair facing the past. Can you see this in your mind's eye? This is called beginning with the end in mind. With your best imagination cap on, answer this question: What do you want to be able to say when you are sitting here at the end of your life? Really, when it comes right down to it, what else matters?

There are two ways I want you to answer this question. To help you, I have rewritten this question with two different focuses on the next page.

Please take a moment to think this through and then write down your responses in the space provided.

One Last Look Beneath the Surface

1. When all is said and done, what do I want to be able to say about me?

_____

_____

_____

_____

2. When all is said and done, what do I want to be said about my family?

_____

_____

_____

_____

Now, take a moment and reflect on your answers. I would even challenge you to pause and get on your knees before your God. Pour out your heart to Him, and talk to Him about your answers to the questions above. Then listen, take in the fullness of His presence in your life, and reflect.

Your *Real* Journey Begins

Thank you for allowing me to share this journey with you. I want to leave you with the words that we began with, paraphrased a bit, but as a reminder of where we have been, and where you are about to go. Below is a brief recap of all that you have read, learned, experienced, and examined. Look it over in its totality to see how far you have come, how brave you have been, and how deep you have allowed the Lord to penetrate.

- You have been challenged to acknowledge and come to terms with a problem that exists for Christian families in our generation in the form of an all-out war for the hearts and minds of our children that must be confronted.

- You have been challenged and equipped to really know your child.

- You have been challenged to grasp the spiritual significance and the historical/scriptural context for where we are in this fight.

- You have challenged to get a hold of hands-on, real-life strategies that will help you parent at the next level.

- You have been challenged to discover and develop the most important factor in next-level parenting—your personal daily walk with Christ.

- You have been challenged to declare your intentions from this moment in history and have learned how you can leave a legacy.

- You have been challenged to develop, in your mind's eye, a picture of what victory looks like and feels like when we parent on purpose, with purpose, and go beyond the norm to a place I call the next level.

T. W. Hunt, a godly man of prayer and wisdom, says this:

Yearning is an intense emotion. Christ's metaphors, *hunger and thirst,* indicate an acute consciousness of need. Later in the Sermon on the Mount, *Jesus tells us to "seek first" God's kingdom and His righteousness* (Matthew 6:33). We are to give priority to that seeking. Jesus is again stressing intensity; one who yearns for righteousness will seek it.... To desire, seek, and pursue righteousness is to align our desires and our activities with those of Christ..."[1]

So get ready to get all the way in for the next few weeks or so. Have the courageous conversations you read about, and then purpose to be the parent God intends you to be. I know it can happen. Commit now to continue the journey you have begun, and God will do the rest.

May God bless and keep you. May the Lord make His face to shine upon you. May the Lord be gracious unto you. May the Lord lift up His countenance upon you, and may He give you peace. I pray that you always have the courage to live and parent at the next level. I leave you with this profound quote from Charles Swindoll, a man I admire greatly.

> I am convinced that strong families are tucked away in pockets of our nations population along hundreds of other back roads, blue highways, and busy cities. They represent places of quiet determination where character is being forged and where our future is being shaped. They do not make the headlines, but it doesn't matter. What does matter is that mothers and dads are staying at the unheralded, relentless, and often thankless task of building their home by wisdom, establishing it by understanding, and, by knowledge, filling each room with precious and pleasant riches.
>
> Enough children reared in places like that will provide all that is needed to turn this nation around. The secret rests with the family…your family and mine.
>
> —CHARLES SWINDOLL

NOTES

INTRODUCTION

1. Abraham Lincoln Online, "Annual Message to Congress—Concluding Remarks," http://showcase.netins.net/web/creative/lincoln/speeches/congress.htm (accessed October 13, 2008).

2. The Barna Group, "Spiritual Progress Hard to Find in 2003," *The Barna Update*, December 22, 2003, http://www.barna.org/FlexPage.aspx?Page=BarnaUpdate&BarnaUpdateID=155 (accessed September 17, 2008).

3. Ibid.

4. The Barna Group, "Parents Accept Responsibility for Their Child's Spiritual Development but Struggle With Effectiveness," *The Barna Update*, May 6, 2003, http://www.barna.org/FlexPage.aspx?Page=BarnaUpdate&BarnaUpdateID=138 (accessed September 17, 2008).

5. Ibid.

1—ADMIT THERE IS A PROBLEM

1. As quoted by Kurt Bruner, "Building a Spiritual Heritage," Dr. Dobson's Monthly Letters, August 2000, FocusontheFamily.com, http://www2.focusonthefamily.com/docstudy/newsletters/A000000262.cfm (accessed September 17, 2008).

2. Beth Moore, *When Godly People Do Ungodly Things* (Nashville, TN: B&H Publishing Group, 2002).

3. Ibid.

4. Lance Morrow, "1968 Like a Knife Blade, the Year Severed Past From Future," *Time*, January 11, 1988, http://www.time.com/time/magazine/article/0,9171,966422,00.html (accessed August 12, 2008).

5. "According to John," *Time*, August 12, 1966, http://www.time.com/time/magazine/article/0,9171,842611,00.html?promoid=googlep (accessed August 12, 2008).

6. Charles Colson and Nancy Pearcey, *The Problem of Evil* (Carol Stream, IL: Tyndale House Publisher, 2001).

2—The Problem Defined

1. Quotedb.com, "C. S. Lewis Quotes," http://www.quotedb.com/quotes/349 (accessed October 13, 2008).

2. Rich Cholodofsky and Richard Gazarik, *Pittsburgh Tribune-Review*, April 30, 2006.

3. Alfe Kohn, "How Not to Teach Values," Phi Delta Kappa, February 1997, http://www.alfiekohn.org/teaching/hnttv.htm (accessed August 13, 2008).

3—The Message of *Next Level Parenting*

1. Quotedb.com, "Dr. Martin Luther King Jr. Quotes," http://www.quotedb.com/quotes/57 (accessed August 13, 2008).

2. Charles Colson, "How Now Shall We Live?" Center for Science and Culture, September 1, 1999, http://www.discovery.org/a/3569 (accessed August 13, 2008).

3. "Children and Young People in a World of AIDS," UNAIDS, 2001, 8, http://data.unaids.org/Publications/IRC-pub02/JC656-Child_Aids_En.pdf (accessed August 14, 2008).

4. "Each Day in America," Children's Defense Fund, March 2008, http://www.childrensdefense.org/site/PageServer?page name=research_national_data_each_day (accessed August 14, 2008).

5. The Barna Group, "Spiritual Progress Hard To Find in 2003," *The Barna Update*, December 22, 2003, http://www.barna.org/FlexPage.aspx?Page=BarnaUpdate&BarnaUpdate ID=155 (accessed August 14, 2008).

6. Abort73.com, "Abortion Statistics," http://www.abort73.com/HTML/II-A-abortion_statistics.html (accessed November 5, 2008).

7. The Barna Group, "Spiritual Progress Hard to Find in 2003."

8. Top Songs of the Week, The Lyric Archive, Week ending 11/29/03. Full list found at Billboard and BPI Communications, http://www.billboard.com/bbcom/index.jsp (accessed October 14, 2008).

9. Parents and Grandparents Alliance (PGA), full-page ad, *Kansas City Star*, section B, page 8, Friday, January 11, 2003.

10. The Barna Group, "Spiritual Progress Hard to Find in 2003."

11. Henry Blackaby, "What Do You See as the Future for the United States?" speech given at the Billy Graham Training Center, Ashville, NC, May 22, 1999.

12. The Barna Group, "Born Again Adults Less Likely to Co-habit, Just as Likely to Divorce," *The Barna Update*, August 6, 2001, http://www.barna.org/FlexPage.aspx?Page=BarnaUpdate&BarnaUpdateID=95 (accessed August 14, 2008).

13. Ibid.

4—STATE OF THE CHRISTIAN FAMILY ADDRESS

1. John Eldredge, *Waking the Dead* (Nashville, TN: Thomas Nelson Publishers, 2003), 13.

2. *Focus on the Family* broadcast, April 20 and 21, 1998, called "What You Learn Could Hurt You." *Comedy and Tragedy*, a booklet produced yearly by the Young America's Foundation. Yearly updates for *Comedy and Tragedy* can be found at www.yaf.org or phone (703)-318-9608.

3. Barna Research statistic quoted at Catalyst Conference Labs, October 2005, Atlanta, Georgia.

4. Dr. David Hager and Dr. Marilyn Maxwell with Dr. Walt Larimore, *Focus on the Family* broadcast, "Answering Women's Health Concerns," March 10, 2004, track 10.

5. The Barna Group, "Research Shows That Spiritual Maturity Process Should Start at a Young Age," *The Barna Update*, November 17, 2003, http://www.barna.org/FlexPage.aspx?Page=BarnaUpdate&BarnaUpdateID=153 (accessed September 17, 2008).

6. Julie Neyman, "Do Evangelical Fathers Really Know Best," *USA Today*, June 16, 2004, http://www.usatoday.com/news/religion/2004-06-16-church-dads_x.htm (accessed August 15, 2008).

7. Ibid.

SECTION II—KNOW YOUR CHILD—ASK THE RIGHT QUESTIONS

1. ThinkExist.com, "John Fitzgerald Kennedy Quotes," http://thinkexist.com/quotation/a_child_miseducated_is_a_child_lost/211011.html (accessed August 15, 2008).

6—CAUSE FOR UNBELIEF (PART 1): IS GOD REAL?

1. BrainyQuote.com, "C. S. Lewis Quotes," http://www.brainyquote.com/quotes/authors/c/c_s_lewis.html (accessed September 4, 2008).

2. Richard Rapaport, "The American Taliban," CommonDreams.org News Center, http://www.commondreams.org/views01/1210-07.htm (accessed November 5, 2008) as published in the *San Francisco Chronicle* on December 10, 2001.

7—CAUSE FOR UNBELIEF (PART 2): NOT YET EXPERIENCED HIS PRESENCE

1. BrainyQuote.com, "Franklin D. Roosevelt Quotes," http://www.brainyquote.com/quotes/authors/f/franklin_d_roosevelt.html (accessed September 4, 2008).

9—CAUSE FOR UNBELIEF (PART 3): THE WORLD IS AN ATTRACTIVE PLACE

1. Benjamin Barber, "America Skips School: Why We Talk So Much About Education and Do So Little," *Harper's* magazine 287, no. 1722 (November 1993): 39. Also available at http://homepages.nyu.edu/~gmp1/barber.htm (accessed September 4, 2008).

2. Kurt Bruner, "Building a Spiritual Heritage," Focus on the Family, August 2005, http://www2.focusonthefamily.com/docstudy/newsletters/A000000262.cfm (accessed September 4, 2008).

3. Dr. Derek Keenan quoting Ravi Zacharias, ACSI Conference, Birmingham, Alabama, February 2004.

10—THE FORK IN THE ROAD

1. QuotesandPoems.com, "Justice," http://www.quotesandpoem.com/quotes/showquotes/subject/justice/4676 (September 17, 2008).

2. Rick Warren, *The Purpose-Driven Life* (Grand Rapids, MI: Zondervan, 2002), 175.

3. David Yount, "Worldwide, Religion Remains the Eternal Growth Industry," *Atlanta Journal-Constitution*, January 13, 2004.

4. David Yount, "Religion Proves to Be an Eternal Growth Industry," *Washington Post*, http://www.integrativespirituality.org/postnuke/html/index.php?name=News&file=article&sid=132 (accessed November 5, 2008).

Section III—Spiritual Significance and Historical Context

1. BrainyQuote.com, "George Santayana Quotes," http://www
.brainyquote.com/quotes/quotes/g/georgesant101521.html
(accessed September 5, 2008).

11—Signs of the Times

1. QuoteWorld.org, "George Orwell Quotes," http://www
.quoteworld.org/quotes/12646 (accessed September 5, 2008).

2. Peg Tyre, Julie Scelfo, and Barbara Kantrowitz, "The
Challenge: Just Say No," *Newsweek*, September 13,
2004, http://www.commonsensemedia.org/resources/
commercialism.php?id=4 (accessed September 9, 2008).

3. Ibid.

4. Ibid.

5. Ibid.

6. Jim Cymbala, *Fresh Wind, Fresh Fire* (Grand Rapids, MI:
Zondervan, 2003).

7. George Barna and Mark Hatch, *Boiling Point* (Ventura, CA:
Regal Books, 2003).

12—The Generational Divide: Beyond the Iron Curtain

1. Haim Ginott, *Teacher and Child: A Book for Parents and Teachers*
(New York, NY: Macmillan, 1972), 13.

2. QuoteWorld.com, "Ralph Waldo Emerson Quotes," http://www.quoteworld.org/quotes/4373 (accessed September 9, 2008).

13—Relationships Matter Most

1. BrainyQuote.com, "Franklin D. Roosevelt Quotes," http://www.brainyquote.com/quotes/quotes/f/franklind132705.html (accessed September 9, 2008).

Section IV—Parenting at the Next Level

1. QuotesandPoem.com, "Success Quotes," http://www.quotesandpoem.com/quotes/showquotes/subject/success/5842 (accessed September 9, 2008).

14—Next-Level Parenting Defined

1. Warren, *The Purpose-Driven Life*.

15—Parenting 101

1. The Barna Group, "Research Shows That Spiritual Maturity Process Should Start at a Young Age," *The Barna Update*, November 17, 2003, http://www.barna.org/FlexPage.aspx?Page=BarnaUpdate&BarnaUpdateID=153 (September 17, 2008).

2. Eldredge, *Waking the Dead*, 1–2.

3.   Rebecca L. Collins, PhD, et al, "Watching Sex on Television Predicts Adolescent Initiation of Sexual Behavior," *Pediatrics* 114, no. 3, (September 2004): e280–e289, http://pediatrics .aappublications.org/cgi/content/full/114/3/e280 (accessed September 11, 2008).

4.   Nancy Ayala, et al, "Reel Life vs. Real Life," *USA Today*, Wednesday, February 13, 2002, front page.

5.   BrainyQuote.com, "George S. Patton Quotes," http://www .brainyquote.com/quotes/authors/g/george_s_patton.html (accessed September 11, 2008).

16—THE FULL ARMOR OF GOD

1.   ThinkExist.com, "Mark Twain Quotes," http://thinkexist .com/quotation/it_is_curious-curious_that_physical_ courage/193977.html (accessed September 11, 2008).

17—PARENTING 201: STANDING IN THE LIGHT

1.   Richard J. Foster, *Celebration of Discipline* (San Francisco: Harper and Row, 1978) as quoted by Charles Swindoll, *Intimacy With the Almighty* (Nashville, TN: J. Countryman, a division of Thomas Nelson, Inc., 1999).

2.   Colson and Pearcey, *The Problem of Evil*, 27.

3.   ThinkExist.com, "Martin Luther King Jr. Quotes," http:// thinkexist.com/quotation/darkness_cannot_drive_out_ darkness-only_light_can/214774.html (accessed September 11, 2008).

4. Family First Aid: Help for Troubled Teens, "Teen Alcohol Use, Underage Drinking and Teen Alcoholism," FamilyFirstAid.com, http://www.familyfirstaid.org/teenalcoholuse.html (accessed November 4, 2008).

5. About.com: Alcoholism, "Are You Addicted," http://alcoholism.about.com (accessed November 4, 2008).

6. Teen Drug Abuse, "Marijuana Use Among Teens," TeenDrugAbuse.us, http://teendrugabuse.us/marijuana.html (accessed November 4, 2008).

7. Teen Drug Abuse, "Statistics on Teen Drug Use," TeenDrugAbuse.us, http://www.teendrugabuse.us/teen_drug_use.html (accessed November 4, 2008).

8. Teen Drug Abuse, "The Health Affects of Teen Alcohol Use," TeenDrugAbuse.us.

9. Oswald Chambers, *My Utmost for His Highest: Selections for the Year* (n.p.: Barbour Publishing, 2000), 11.

18—PARENTING 301: THE "ME" FACTOR

1. Charles Swindoll, *The Strong Family: Masculine Model of Leadership* (Portland, OR: Multnomah Publishing, 1991), 31.

2. Thom Reiner, "The Top Ten Fears of Our Youth," Building Church Leaders, http://www.buildingchurchleaders.com/articles/2005/072605.html (accessed November 4, 2008).

3. Parents. The Anti-Drug, "The Parenting of Teens," TheAntiDrug.com, http://www.theantidrug.com/advice/parenting.asp (accessed November 4, 2008).

Section V—Declare Your Intentions

1. ThinkExist.com, "Thomas Jefferson Quotes," http://thinkexist.com/quotation/do_you_want_to_know_who_you_are-don-t_ask-act/225646.html (accessed September 12, 2008).

19—Prepare Your Heart

1. Warren, *The Purpose Driven Life*.

2. QuoteWorld.com, "Abraham Lincoln Quotes," http://www.quoteworld.org/quotes/8315 (accessed September 12, 2008).

20— Truth and Consequences

1. Jentezen Franklin, *Fasting* (Lake Mary, FL: Charisma House, 2008).

2. Darlene Zschech, *Extravagant Worship* (Grand Rapids, MI: Bethany House, 2004).

3. Jim Cymbala with Stephen Sorenson, *The Church God Blesses* (Grand Rapids, MI: Zondervan, 2002), 35.

21—The Rest of the Story

1. Henry Blackaby, *Experiencing God Workbook* (Nashville, TN: LifeWay Press, 1990).

2. Rich Rogers, *Common Parenting Practices and Strategies of Parents of Very Successful High School Seniors*, EdD Dissertation, Pepperdine University GSEP, July, 2000.

3. BrainyQuote.com, "C. S. Lewis Quotes," http://www
.brainyquote.com/quotes/authors/c/c_s_lewis.html (accessed
September 17, 2008).

22—As For Me and My House...

1. Henry Blackaby and Kerry L. Skinner, *Created to be God's
Friend Workbook* (Nashville, TN: Thomas Nelson Publishers,
2000), 77.

Section VI—A People of Joy With Children of Hope

1. Martin Luther King Jr., "Letter From a Birmingham Jail,"
January 3, 1964, http://www.time.com/time/magazine/
article/0,9171,940761-2,00.html (accessed September 16,
2008).

24—What If?

1. ThinkExist.com, "Thomas Jefferson Quotes," http://
thinkexist.com/quotation/every_generation_needs_a_new_
revolution/225819.html (accessed September 17, 2008).

25—Begin With the End in Mind

1. BrainyQuote.com, "Abraham Lincoln Quotes," http://www
.brainyquote.com/quotes/authors/a/abraham_lincoln.html
(accessed September 16, 2008).

26—WHAT'S LEFT TO DO?

1. Charles Colson, *The Problem of Evil* (Carol Stream, IL: Tyndale House Publishers, Inc., 1999).

2. Kathleen Dougherty, "Building an Ethical Community: An Interview with Michael Josephson," *Hemisphere* magazine, August 1996, 21–26.

27—THE MILLION-DOLLAR QUESTION

1. T. W. Hunt, *The Mind of Christ*, (Nashville, TN: Broadman and Holman Publishers, 1995), 83.

2. Charles Swindoll, *The Strong Family* (Portland, OR: Multnomah Press, 1991).

Dr. Rich is available for special events or speaking engagements, and additional Next Level products, articles, and blogs are available online.

Please visit www.RichRogers.org or www.NextLevelUniversity.org for all your Next Level needs and to book Dr. Rich at your next event!
Phone: (407) 514-6143 or (404) 468-0816
E-mail: rogers006@cox.net

DISCOVER LIFE
AT THE
NEXT LEVEL

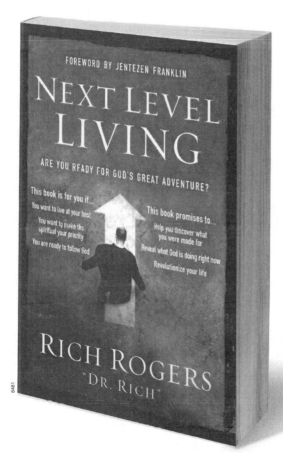

In *Next Level Living*, Dr. Rich walks you through a five-step process that will move you from your current life to a place of incredible significance, influence, and purpose.

Are you ready for God's great adventure?

978-1-59979-197-5
$14.99

VISIT YOUR
LOCAL BOOKSTORE.

Charisma
HOUSE
A STRANG COMPANY

FREE NEWSLETTERS
TO HELP EMPOWER YOUR LIFE

Why subscribe today?

☐ **DELIVERED DIRECTLY TO YOU.** All you have to do is open your inbox and read.

☐ **EXCLUSIVE CONTENT.** We cover the news overlooked by the mainstream press.

☐ **STAY CURRENT.** Find the latest court rulings, revivals, and cultural trends.

☐ **UPDATE OTHERS.** Easy to forward to friends and family with the click of your mouse.

CHOOSE THE E-NEWSLETTER THAT INTERESTS YOU MOST:

- Christian news
- Daily devotionals
- Spiritual empowerment
- And much, much more

SIGN UP AT: **http://freenewsletters.charismamag.com**

8178